Security English

Myungyung Kim and Hongsup Shin

HONGICK PUBLISHING

CONTENTS

Chapter 1 Security Equipment ········· 1
Chapter 2 Patrolling ········· 11
Chapter 3 Security Guard ········· 21
Chapter 4 Detail Security ········· 31
Chapter 5 Detail Security Motorcade ········· 41
Chapter 6 Escort: Carrying Valuables ········· 51
Chapter 7 Escort: Carrying a Firearm ········· 61
Chapter 8 Safety of Persons ········· 71
Chapter 9 Advance Security ········· 81
Chapter 10 Advance Security Site Security ········· 91
Chapter 11 Security at the Airport ········· 101
Chapter 12 Air Trip ········· 111
Chapter 13 Control Crowds ········· 121
Chapter 14 Emergency ········· 131
Chapter 15 Transportation ········· 141

❖ SECURITY ENGLISH TERMINOLOGY ········· 151

Chapter 1

Security Equipment

Welcome and getting to know each other

Making the business card

Make your own business card (Name, Position, Address, Telephone numbers, email address, Company name, etc.) and introduce yourself to your colleagues and collect seven peoples' personal information from their name cards.

The Security Uniform

Uniforms are an excellent item and serve several functions. They usually comprise of a shirt with shoulder insignia or epaulettes identifying the organization, twin breast pockets for notebooks and pens, trousers, utility belt for carrying equipment and of course shoes.

Uniforms are universally recognized as a symbol of authority, identify the wearers company or organization of origin and present a professional appearance. By design, they enable the wearers to carry a number of otherwise difficult to manage tools and devices, with greater ease and comfort.

Epaulettes
장교견장
Equipment and Facilities
장비 및 시설
Shoulder Insignia
어깨견장
Uniformed Police
정복경찰

The Torch

Torches are an absolutely essential piece of security equipment. When working nights a torch will enable you to identify damage to client's property, spot hazardous or unsafe situations and areas, light your path and identify offenders.

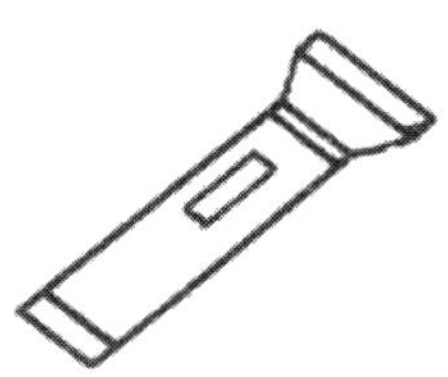

The Notebook

A security officer really cannot operate without one, and the notebook itself is useless unless you also have a pen that works!

Torch
손전등
Security Equipment
경호장비
Clients Property
고객자산
Offender
침입자

The 2 Way Radio (Walkie-Talkie)

The two way radio is a very important piece of equipment. The two-way radio is still the preferred system of communication for most large security firms. This mode of communication is cheaper than mobile phone use and is more versatile for a company with many mobile officers on patrol.

The Alpha Code

A	ALPHA
B	BRAVO
C	CHARLIE
D	DELTA
E	ECHO
F	FOXTROT
G	GOLF
H	HOTEL
I	INDIA
J	JULIET
K	KILO
L	LIMA
M	MIKE
N	NOVEMBER
O	OSCAR
P	PAPA
Q	QUEBEC
R	ROMEO
S	SIERRA
T	TANGO
U	UNIFORM
V	VICTOR
W	WHISKY
X	X-RAY
Y	YANKEE
Z	ZULU

Nice to meet you.

When you introduce people, remember these things.

1. *Look at the people you are introducing.*
2. *Say the names of each person.*
3. *Tell something about each person.*

Bill:	Hello. My name is Bill.
Jennifer:	Hi. I'm Jennifer.
	Nice to meet you.
Bill:	Nice to meet you, too.
Jennifer:	Good morning.
	My name is Jennifer.
John:	Hello. My name is John.
	I'm glad to meet you.
Jennifer:	Glad to meet you, too.

What's your name?

Bob:	What's your name?
Susan:	My name is Susan.
	What's your name?
Bob:	My name is Bob.
	What's your first name?
Susan:	My first name is Susan.
	What's your first name?
Bob:	My first name is Bob.
Susan:	What's your last name?
Bob:	My last name is Mercer.
Susan:	Please spell that.
Bob:	M-E-R-C-E-R.

You often speak to two or more people at the same time. Sometimes they may not know each other. You may need to introduce them.

Robert's mother has come to Parent's Day at school. She has never met his teacher. Let's see how Robert introduces his mother to his teacher.

"Mr. Weber, I'd like you to meet my mother, Mrs. Lee."

Then Robert turns to his mother. He says, "Mom, this is my teacher, Mr. Weber. He has been helping me learn to write better".

First, Robert presented his mother to his teacher. He introduced his mother by saying her name. Next, Robert introduced his teacher, Mr. Weber. He also told his mother something about his teacher. You should always say more than names when you introduce people. Try to think of something interesting to say about each person. This will make it easier for people to start talking.

Where do you live?

Carrying on a Conversation

When you are having a conversation, listen carefully, answer politely, and ask questions.

Once people know something about each other, they usually begin to talk. However, carrying on a conversation is not always easy. You must keep your mind on what people are saying. It is important to listen and ask questions.

Sally: Where do you live?

Mark: I live in New York.
How about you, Sally?

Sally: I live in Denver, Colorado.

Mark: Where does Judy live?

Sally: She lives in Denver, too.
Mark, what part of New York do you live?

Mark: I live on the east side.

Are you married?

Guides for Carrying on a Conversation

1. Let each person talk.
2. Ask questions.
3. Add new ideas.
4. Listen to others.
5. Be friendly.

Donald: Are you married?

Susan: Yes, I am.

Donald: Is he married?

Susan: No, he isn't. He's single.

Donald: Is she married?

Susan: Yes, she is. She's married.

Are they married?

Donald: Yes, they are. They are married.

They're happy.

Fill in the following information about your partner.

What's your name?

My name is ____________.

How do you come to school?

I come to school by ________.

How many people are there in your family?

There are __________ people in my family.

Do you play tennis?

Yes, I do. / No, I don't, but I ________.

What's your favorite food?

My favorite food is __________.

Fill in the following information about your partner.

B Student

What's your name?

My name is ________.

What's your student number?

My student number is __________.

How old are you?

I'd rather not say. / I'm _____ years old.

Do you like soccer?

Yes, I do. / No, I don't, but I like _______.

Who's your favorite actor?

My favorite actor is _______.

Chapter 2

Patrolling

Patrolling

Australian ISF soldiers on patrol in Dili

The primary function of security is the protection of people and property. One of the most significant protection weapons possessed by the security industry is that of the mobile person.

Effective security is the providing of a professional service that ensures protection of the client and the client's property, through regular patrol activities or duties. Patrol duties are periodic inspections of various premises either on foot or by motor vehicle.

Patrolling is a military tactic. Small groups or individual units are deployed from a larger formation to achieve a specific objective and then return. The tactic of patrolling may apply to ground troops, armored units, naval units, and combat aircraft. The duration of a patrol can vary from a few hours to several weeks depending on the nature of the objective and the type of units involved

Patrol Techniques

Patrol routes and starting points should be varied and changed frequently to ensure the element of surprise and to prevent a pattern of your movements being determined by offenders.

Time is money, and the last thing a patrol person needs to do is have their patrol routes cross upon themselves, it's a time waster.

Base should be notified via two way radio if pre-arranged routes have to be changed.

To do this you must ensure that effective communications have been established with your security office and all incidents reported and all patrol times recorded in patrol book.

Incidents
사건
Mobile Person
순찰대원
Offenders
침입자
Patrol duties
순찰의무
Patrol Routes
순찰경로
Premises
건물, 부동산
Property
재산

Patrol Procedure

* If it is an intruder and appears dangerous, DO NOT attempt to overpower him or her.
* Keep out of the way and radio for assistance.
* Place yourself in a suitable vantage point and wait for the police to arrive.
* If an arrest situation occurs use as much force as is absolutely necessary, at the time, to effect a lawful arrest (i.e. Reasonable Force).
* Be exact in the wording you use to arrest a person.
* Record any conversation you have with the offender in your notebook in first person, I said, ~~~~, He/She said ~~~
* Do not delay in calling the police.
* Write up your report from the notes you made at the time of the occurrence.
* Do not place yourself or others at risk.
* Be alert at all times.

Intruder
침입자
Occurrence
발생
Overpower
압도하다
Radio
무전기
Vantage Point
유리한 지점

Preparation for Patrol

* Your uniform or clothes are clean, neat, pressed and tidy.
* Footwear is clean and polished.
* Pockets of uniform jacket or shirt are buttoned.
* Tie is clean and straight.
* Be clean shaven.
* Fingernails are clean.
* You have security license.
* Your torch is in good working condition.
* You have your baton and handcuffs (if required)
* You have your notebook.
* You have a couple of working pens or biros.

Scrambled Words

There are some problems with the sound track. Fix the scrambled words.

1. Your othcr is in good working condition.
2. You have security cliseen.
3. Your uniform or clothes are cnela, neat, pressed and tidy.
4. You have your nkotoeob.
5. Do not deayl in calling the police.
6. Do not place yourself or others at ikrs.
7. Be aterl at all times.
8. Keep out of the way and oraid for assistance.
9. Place yourself in a suitable vantage point and wait for the opicle to arrive.
10. Be exact in the wording you use to rarets a person.
11. aptrlo
12. haffncdus
13. otnvsreacion
14. effonedr
15. pryrepot
16. prttnoecio
17. mboeil
18. wpeona

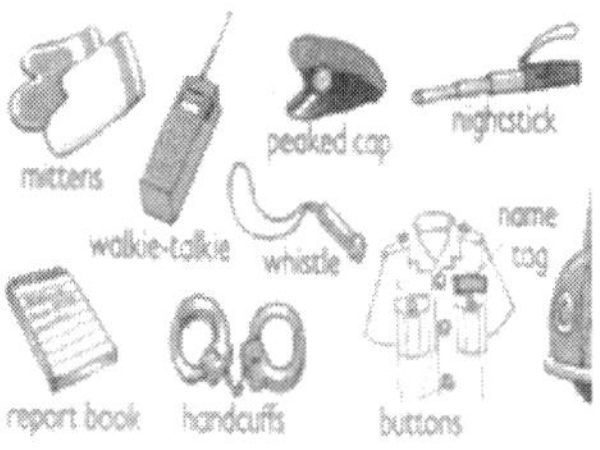

Where are you from?

Mary: Where are you from?

Donald: I'm from Germany.

Where are you from?

Mary: I'm from Mexico.

What country is he from?

Donald: He's from Korea.

Mary: What city is he from?

Donald: He's from Daegu.

Mary: What's his address?

Donald: His address is 77 Main Street.

Mary: What's his phone number?

Donald: His phone number is 567-4289.

How old are you?

Judy: How old are you?

Gary: I'm 22 years old.

Judy: What's your birth date?

Gary: It's July 18, 1994.

How old is Dan?

Judy: He's 20.

Gary: What's his birth date?

Judy: It's May 25, 1994.

CROSSWORD PUZZLE

(Across)

2. What's your phone number?
My ______ number is 777-6969.
4. I live in Hayward, ____ San Francisco.
6. How are you? I'm not too bad. _____ you.
8. It's _____ to meet you, Jennifer. Nice to meet you, too.
10. What's your ____ name?
My name is Dave.
11. Where are you _____?
I'm from Germany.
13. Where _____ Susan live? She lives in Dallas.

(Down)

1. ____ in Dallas do you live?
I live near the airport.
2. I live in New York. What ____ of New York. I live on the west side.
3. I was __ on Dec. 4, 1990.
5. I live ____ Seattle.
7. My ____ is 7 Main Street.
9. Where do you come from, Brad? I _____ from Canada.
12. How are you? Not _____ good.

Adverbs of Frequency

Walk around the classroom and ask your classmates these questions. Put their name and how often in thc blanks. Choose your answers from the list of adverbs below.

Do you ever .... ?	Name
1. go to the public bath?	______
2. swim at the beach?	______
3. shoot pool in the evening?	______
4. crochet?	______
5. lift weights?	______
6. horror films?	______
7. take the subway?	______
8. go on camping trip?	______
9. eat raw fish?	______
10. cook dinner at home?	______
11. clean your bedroom?	______
12. eat deep fried squid?	______

Adverbs of frequency

Everyday
Sometimes
Always
Hardly ever
Almost always
Usually
Twice a week
Once a year
Three times a month
Never
Often
Occasionally
Once a week

Reading

Dear Tina,

How are you? My name is Paul Lee. I was born on April 23, 1990. I am from Korea, but I live in Oregon. I am a student at State College. My major is international trade. On Sundays, I study Spanish. I work part time at a restaurant near my home. I'm not married and I do not have a girl friend yet. In my free time, I like to go fishing. I also like walking on Oregon's beautiful beaches. How about you? What do you do? Do you have any hobbies? I hope you will write soon.

Your friend,

Paul

What does Paul do in his free time?

1. He likes girlfriends and swimming at the beach.
2. He is a student.
3. He likes walking and fishing.
4. He doesn't have hobbies.

Chapter 3

Security Guard

Security Guard

The term Security Guard is derived from security personnel performing this activity and such security guards represent a major proportion of manpower services within the security industry.

Guard duties cover such areas of activity as static guard posts, bank duties and watching or guarding a building group of buildings. Access control is all about regulating entry into and in some cases exit from, security controlled premises. Access control is accomplished in part by limiting access to premises and overseeing entry of persons and or vehicles.

Overall guard duties are for the protection of structures, equipment and personnel and personal property thereon from fire, flood, vandalism, trespass, mechanical malfunction, personal threat and all such dangers.

Security Guard
경호원
Static Guard
초소경비원
Access Control
출입통제
Premises
건물, 부동산
Vehicle
차량
Vandalism
예술문화파괴
Trespass
불법침입
Malfunction
기능부전

Gate Control

Gatehouse duties require the security officer to become familiar with the various organisational procedures. You must know all the various passes used, and be able to make accurate log book entries efficiently. The process of checking and rechecking the various passes, vehicles and cargo will take up a large portion of the gate controllers time.

Gate Control Procedure

* Check that the pass shown is for the person or vehicle described.
* Ensure that all vehicles entering are provided with the appropriate pass or semi- permanent company issued pass.
* Ensure that only authorised employees' and visitors' vehicles use designated inside parking areas.
* Ensure that employees' vehicles display an appropriate authority to use designated inside parking areas.
* Ensure that ALL persons occupying a goods vehicle etc., have an appropriate separate company pass or I.D. card.
* Ensure all goods' vehicles present the correct documentation.
* Ensure that all goods, delivery, service or contractor vehicles are properly logged.
* Make sure that all visitors to the premises fill in the visitor's book correctly and sign it.

I.D. Card
신분증
Parking Areas
주차지역
Vehicle
차량

How are you?

Jennifer:	Good morning, Bill.
Bill:	Hello, Jennifer. How are you?
Jennifer:	I am great, thank you.
	And how are you?
Bill:	I'm not too bad. Thanks.
Jennifer:	How is she?
Bill:	She's busy. How are they?
Jennifer:	They are fine.

How is John?

Bob: How is John?

Susan: He's tired.

Bob: How are Sue and Joe?

Susan: They're happy.

Bob: How is Jennifer?

Susan: She's busy.

Bob: How is Fred?

Susan: He's angry.

* Match

*** Match**

Fine

Busy

Tired

Hot

Cold

Happy

Sad

Angry

Nervous

I'm sick.

Sally: How are you?

Mark: I'm sick.

Sally: What's the matter?

Mark: I have a cold.

Sally: Do you have a fever?

Mark: Yes, I have. I am not going to school.

Sally: I hope you feel better.

* Look at the pictures and respond the way these people would.

1. They have ____________.

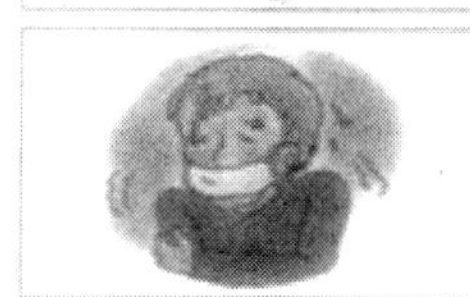

2. He has a ____________.

3. He has a ________ ________.

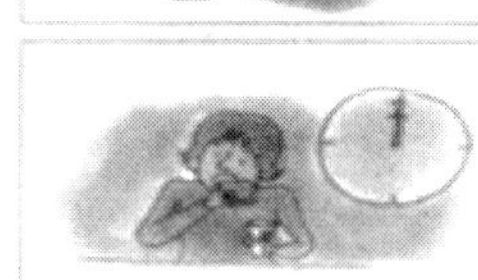

4. She has a ________ ________.

Interview

* Find out if your friend is healthy.

* Add up the points and figure it out.

□Never (3 points) □Sometimes (2 points)

□Quite often (1 points) □Often (0 points)

1. How often do you have a headache?

□Never □Sometimes □Quite often □Often

2. How often do you have a stomachache?

□Never □Sometimes □Quite often □Often

3. How often do you have a backache?

□Never □Sometimes □Quite often □Often

4. How often do you have a toothache?

□Never □Sometimes □Quite often □Often

5. How often do you have the flu?

□Never □Sometimes □Quite often □Often

6. How often do you have a fever?

□Never □Sometimes □Quite often □Often

7. How often do you have a sore throat?

□Never □Sometimes □Quite often □Often

8. How often do you have a earache?

□Never □Sometimes □Quite often □Often

Points 20-24
You're very healthy.
You're in great shape.

Points 12-19
You're quite healthy. Keep up the good work.

Points 7-11
Get more exercise and eat lots of fruits and vegetables.

Points 0-6
You aren't healthy. Go and see a doctor.

The Body

Match

Hair

Eye

Ear

Nose

Mouth

Chin

Neck

Shoulder

Chest

Arm

Elbow

Stomach

Wrist

Hand

Finger

Knee

Leg

Ankle

Foot

Toe

Find someone who...

1. Can you swim? Name: ______
2. Can you cook well? Name: ______
3. Can you ride a bicycle? Name: ______
4. Can you play golf? Name: _____
5. Do you like pizza? Name: _____.
6. Do you smoke? Name: _____
7. Do you like to drink? Name: _____
8. Are you hungry? Name: _____
9. Are you a baseball fan? Name: _____
10. Do you like pizza? Name: _____.

Chapter 4

Detail Security

Detail Protection

Jennifer: Please let us know of the number of your personnel and the escort formation at the time of detail security in addition any plans for combined duty with our personnel.

Bill: For detail security, we plan to combine with your personnel, and will utilize from five to seven Secret Service agents of our own to be placed in a diamond or a box formation for regular walking alignment.

Jennifer: How many detail security agents will you use?

Bill: 6 men, in diamond formation.

Jennifer: How many of our men can be used for detail security?

Bill: 4 of your men can be present.

Jennifer: Can you let us know beforehand of movement routes for each event site?

Bill: We're extending them to 2 or 3 routes, and will decide on them the morning of the event.

Detail Security
근접경호
Escort Formation
호위대형
Walking Alignment
도보대형
Movement Route
기동로
Dignitary Protective Division
요인경호과

Road Security

Jennifer: What are your plans for traffic control during the movement of our VIP vehicles?

Bill: We plan to proceed non-stop from point to point, and prefer a Frog-Jump style method for momentary control at intersection.

Jennifer: Please inform us of the time for deciding to-and-from travel routes.

Bill: Those decisions are made by the Secret Service as per various circumstances, and we will inform you in advance in case any changes are necessary.

Jennifer: Can you tell us about the security measures along the VIP travel route?

Bill: Uniformed police officers will be situated at intersections, corners, and vulnerable areas, while snipers will be used to cover any buildings that have a direct shot.

Jennifer: Please inform us concerning whether there are plans for the inspection of the main routes of travel.

Bill: The motorcade route will be patrolled by squad cars, prior to the VIP motorcade and we are making sure there are no suspicious weaknesses to the access routes.

Jennifer: Please inform us concerning plans for the use of aerial security by helicopter along travel route.

Bill: We regularly use helicopters for aerial security during the movement between official event sites.

Uniformed police
정복경찰
Vulnerable areas
취약지역
Sniper
저격병
Motorcade route
차량기동로
Squad cars
경찰기동차량
Access route
진입로
Aerial security
공중경호

Roadside Security

Jennifer: Who has the plan for roadside security?

Bill: I do, ma'am. Tony has the size of force and the disposition of force.

Jennifer: Okay then. Tony, have you set up alternate routes for the presidential motorcade?

Tony: Yes, I have. All security arrangements are being made.

Sam: Traffic control is being monitored at the safety room on the route.

Bill: Tony and I will check on pavement conditions today.

Tony: Downtown buildings are being blockaded two hours before arrival of the motorcade.

Sam: All vulnerable areas downtown will also be monitored starting two hours before motorcade.

Jennifer: Fantastic, guys! Sounds like you are on top of things.

Roadside Security
연도경호
Disposition of Force
병력배치
Alternate Routes
예비통로
Pavement Condition
도로포장상태

Escort

Jennifer: Please let us know of the number of personnel and the escort formation at the time of detail security.

Bill: We plan to utilize five to seven Secret Service agents to be utilized at regular walking alignment.

Jennifer: Are all emergency measure taken care of?

Bill: Yes. We have the designation of the nearest hospital from each site and we have an employment of an ambulance at our service.

Jennifer: Good. Let's make sure we have protection while walking and if something happens remember protocol.

What are you looking for?

Bob: What are you looking for?

Susan: I'm looking for my backpack.

Bob: Look, it's under the desk.

Susan: Oh, yeah. There it is.

But, where is my math book?

Bob: Isn't it in the backpack?

Susan: No, it isn't.

Bob: Oh, it is behind the desk.

Susan: Thank you.

Where are they?

* Talk to your friend where they are and what they are doing.

Where can I buy a ticket?

Donald: Excuse me.

Where can I buy a ticket?

Kevin: Are you looking for the ticket office?

Donald: Yes, I am.

I want the ticket office.

Kevin: It's next to the drug store.

Donald: Sorry. How do I get there?

Kevin: Go straight ahead, and it's on the right.

Donald: OK. Thanks for your help.

Scrambled Words

Fix the scrambled words.

1. The car is in the agareg. garage
2. My mother is at the torpair. ______
3. My favorite room is the kcethin. ______
4. They're in the hlosatip. ______
5. Mark is in the stop coffie. ______
6. All the students are in the rsepuktmera. ______
7. Is Susan in the rblariy. ______
8. Carmen is in the bekayr. ______
9. Kevin is in the rsarntetua. ______
10. Fred is in the rakp. ______

Chapter 5

Detail Security Motorcade

Motorcade Formation

Jennifer: Who will take a ride on the VIP car?

Bill: He is ADC (Aide-de-camp)

Jennifer: How much gas is left?

Bill: The fuel tank is full.

Jennifer: Stand by a car at this place at 6 o'clock in the morning, please.

Bill: We'll do it.

Jennifer: Concerning the vehicles being provided for our President and First Lady, please inform us of the made and model, and also whether it is bullet-proof.

Bill: Each of the vehicles being provided for your President and First Lady will be a bullet proof limousine.

Jennifer: Who will be responsible for the opening and closing of our President's car door at the time of arrival and departure from the event sites?

Bill: Our Secret Service personnel will be wholly responsible for that.

ADC (Aide-De-Camp)
부관
Bulletproof
방탄
Event Site
행사장

Jennifer: Can you let us know the details of the motorcade alignment?

Bill: You can refer to this map for the motorcade alignment along each section of the route.

Jennifer: We would like to have the PSS chief's vehicle positioned as the initial vehicle of the attendants.

Bill: We'll see to it then.

Jennifer: Can you tell us something about plans for the operation of VIP vehicles, and about an emergency stand-by area?

Bill: We will have VIP vehicles on H-20 prior stand-by, the stand-by area is the White House parking lot, and we will have two vehicles stationed at the front of the Blair House for emergency stand-by.

Motorcade Alignment
차량정렬
PSS(Presidential Security Service) 대통령경호실
Stand-by Area
대기지역
Emergency Stand-by
비상대기

Motorcade Advance

Alternate Routes
예비통로
Lead Car
선도차량
Reserve Car
예비차
Vehicle Chart
차량편성표

Jennifer: Let's go through the itinerary for the presidential conference of Asia. Are you ready?

Bill: Yes, I am.

Jennifer: Do you have the alternate route planned?

Bill: Check. All routed.

Jennifer: Are preventive measures taken for possible terrorist attacks?

Bill: Written down, practiced and in place, ma'am.

Jennifer: How about the lead car?

Bill: Check.

Jennifer: The reserve car?

Bill: Check.

Jennifer: The list of doctors?

Bill: Check.

Jennifer: Stand by car?

Bill: Check.

Jennifer: Vehicle chart?

Bill: Check.

Jennifer: Traffic control?

Bill: Check.

Jennifer: It sounds like you have everything checked out.

Bill: Check.

Detail Security Motorcade

Jennifer: What's the type of VIP vehicle?

Bill: It's a 2010 Equus with bulletproof windows.

Jennifer: Is the seating arrangement for security agents in the car set up?

Bill: Yes. There will be three, one in the front and two in the back with the First lady.

Jennifer: Good. Is the reserve car arranged?

Bill: Yes. We also have the motorcycles scheduled.

Jennifer: How about the seating arrangement in the conference hall?

Bill: Everything is taken care of. It is set up according to the keep left system and the PSS chief's seat will be two seats to the left of the First lady.

Jennifer: Who will open the door of the VIP vehicle?

Bill: That will be me sir, because I will also be in charge of the counter measures against an emergency.

Jennifer: I knew I could count on you an Agent Bond.

Seat Arrangement
좌석배치
Countermeasures
대처방법

What are you doing?

Bob: Hi, Susan. How are you today?

Susan: Very good. What are you doing?

Bob: I'm playing cards.

Susan: What is your sister doing?

Bob: She's making dinner right now.

Susan: What is your brother doing?

Bob: He is reading a book.
How about you?

Susan: I'm going to the library.

What are you doing on the weekend?

Bob: What are you doing on the weekend?

Susan: I'm working at my part-time job on Saturday. What are you doing on the weekend?

Bob: I'm doing my laundry. Would you like to go to the movies on Sunday night?

Susan: I'm sorry, I can't.
I'm doing the housework.

Match Excuses

- Working overtime.
- Going to a concert.
- Fixing the sink.
- Visiting relatives
- Babysitting.
- Doing exercise.
- Washing my clothes.
- Studying math.
- Making dinner.

WEEKDAYS

SUNDAY

MONDAY

TUESDAY

WEDNESDAY

THURSDAY

FRIDAY

SATURDAY

My Schedule

- Write or draw your daily activities.
- Find a classmate for each activity.
- Compare your grid and your partner's grid.
- What is the same? What is different?

Time/Date	Morning	Afternoon	Evening	Night
Sunday				
Monday				
Tuesday				
Wednesday				
Thursday				
Friday				
Saturday				

Watch TV
Play the piano
Read newspaper
Ride a bicycle
Play baseball
Go fishing
Write a letter
Play the violin
Play the guitar
Play the cello
Play the drums
Do homework
Wash my face
Brush my teeth
Go swimming
Sing a song
Listen to music
Comb my hair
Read a book
Have breakfast
Have lunch
Have dinner
Go to the movies
Climb mountains
Play tennis

What are they doing?

Bob: What are they doing?

Susan: I'm studying math.

What are you doing?

Bob: I'm studying science.

What is Andy doing?

Susan: He's playing baseball.

What is Carol doing?

Bob: She's washing her clothes.

What is John doing?

Susan: He's fixing the car.

What is Victor doing?

Bob: He's watching TV.

What are Nancy and John doing?

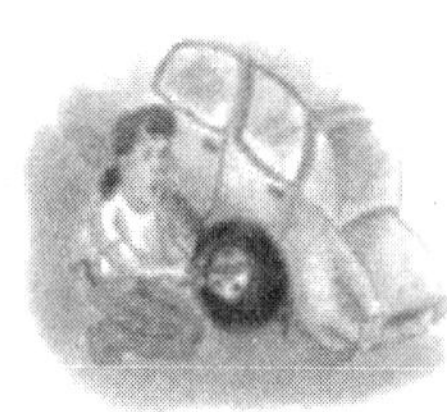

Susan: They're preparing for a picnic.

Crossword Puzzle

(Across)

2. I'm ________ to go to hiking with Nancy.
3. Mr. Jones is _______ the newspaper.
5. The birds are ________.
7. Judy loves _______ a new blouse.
8. They are _______ English.

(Down)

1. She's _________ lunch.
2. Tommy Jones is _________ the guitar.
4. Susan is ________ her homework.
6. I'm ________ to meet a friend and have coffee.

Chapter 6

Escort: Carry Valuables

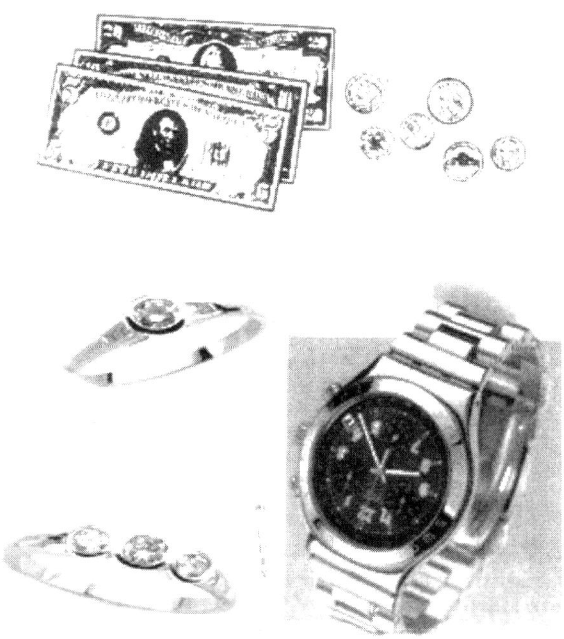

Escort and Carry Valuables

Cash escorts or escorts of valuable objects and materials are perhaps the highest risk areas in the security industry. It is essential that security officers be aware of the various dangers they may encounter at any time during the escorts.

The various resources required for this type of activity include:

1. Trained licensed (both class 1 and firearms) personnel
2. Reliable communication equipment
3. Motor vehicles (both armoured, marked and unmarked)
4. Firearms
5. Portable safe deposit boxes

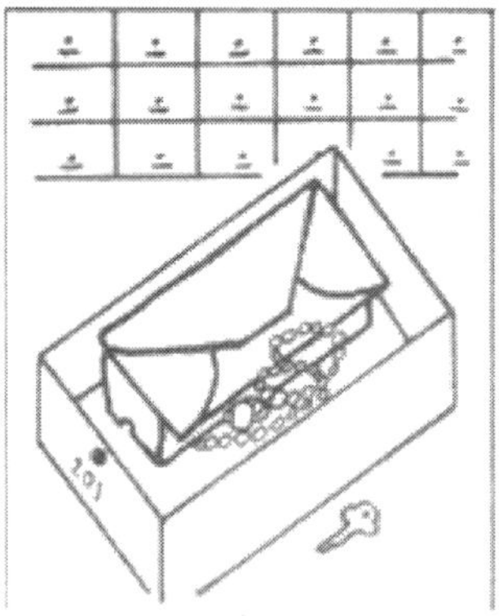

When preparing for an escort and carrying valuables (Large sums of money, payrolls, gold or silver bullion and other precious metals, diamonds and other gem stones, jewellery, rare artefacts and antiques) a checklist should include the following:

1. Ensure that all equipment is in full working order (check and test two way radios, check firearms are loaded).
2. Ensure that all vehicles are serviced and fuelled.
3. Safest most direct route determined and mapped out.
4. All paperwork (invoices etc) on hand.
5. Spotter vehicles and other crew briefed on procedures.

Valuables
귀중품
Firearms
총기
Gold bullion
금괴

VARIOUS ROLES

The escorting valuables is as follows, a driver of the main transport (probably armored) vehicle, Observer and navigator in cabin with driver, Guards (protection for cargo), lookout/s (shotgun), both in armored vehicle and in spot vehicle, and Driver for spot vehicle.

Upon arrival at the receiving station the following things should be remembered:

1. Ensure that weapons can be easily accessed by a free hand.
2. Be aware of other traffic en route, watch for tails.
3. Maintain a constant lookout when entering or existing an escort vehicle.
4. Always check area before payroll officer exits vehicle, drive on if something suspicious is present, you can always return when safe.
5. If riding shotgun with the escort vehicle, exit your vehicle prior to those on the cash van. Stand in a position away from vehicle to provide a better field of view, do not open doors for them as your job is protection.

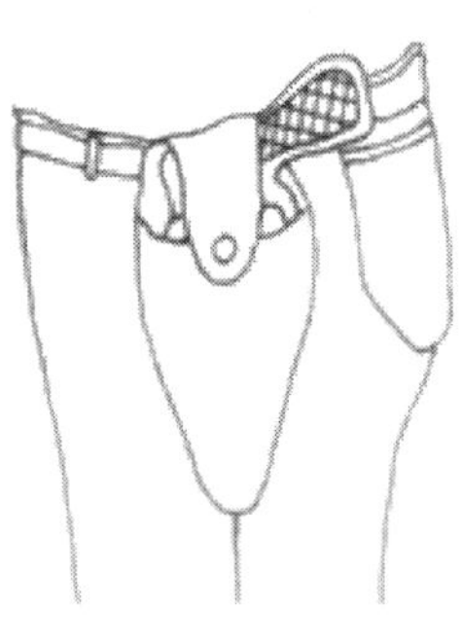

6. Check all alleys and entrances to buildings.
7. Always remain alert and stay in communication.
8. Be aware of surrounds and numbers of civilians the in area.
9. If escorting, stand where you can observe and protect.
10. Report anything unusual.
11. Do not assist destination staff as this restricts you from performing your function, which is to keep a constant lookout.
12. Be aware that the prime times for a hit (ie most dangerous) are when entering and exiting the transport vehicle.
13. Take note of unusually parked vehicles (eg 'getaway vehicles') and record rego numbers and descriptions.
14. Identify possible hiding places.
15. Check identification of any persons you deal with if you do not know them.
16. Note possible escape routes.

GENERAL RULES

1. Where possible vary route, pick up time, and deposit time.
2. Do not get involved in distracting conversation.
3. Do not discuss confidential work details with people who do not need to know.
4. Carry your firearm with access to it by your strong hand where possible.
5. Make body language strong not weak (thieves prefer a 'weak' target).
6. Sit in the front of the vehicle where you have a better field of view.
7. For larger sums of money or valuables have two or more escorting the valuables.
8. Be careful of giving advice to the client as there are legal liability implications.

Practical Conversations

Hotel Reservations

- Do you have any room?
- I'll stay for three nights.
- I'd like to reserve a double room for the 14th.
- I'd like to make a reservation for five nights for two.
- I'd like a single room with a bath, please.
- What's the rate for a room per night?
- Is breakfast included in this rate?
- I need to change my reservation.
- Will you fill in this registration form, please?

Hotel Checkout

Tom: Excuse me, I'd like to check out now. How much is the room charge?

Brad: Just a moment, please. Your bill comes to 80 dollars including the tax and the service charge.

Tom: Can I pay with a traveler's check?

Brad: That will be fine, sir.

Hotel Room Service

- How do I call room service?
- Could you please send up coffee for two to Room 403?
- Please bring my breakfast to my room.
- Could you rush the order?
- Please give me a wake-up call tomorrow morning at 7 o'clock.
- Would you make the bed while I am out?
- This is room 110. Do you have a message for me?
- I sent my dress out to be cleaned, but it hasn't come back yet.
- I locked myself out.
- I'd like to extend my stay for a few days.
- May I have a late checkout?

Restaurant Reservations

- Please reserve a table for three at eight tonight.
- I'm sorry, but the seats are full at that time.
- Do you have a table for two?
- I called for a reservation for 7 o'clock this evening.
- Your name isn't on the list.
- We'd prefer to sit in the non-smoking section.
- How long do we have to wait?

Restaurant Ordering

- I'd like to coffee before the meal.
- What's the chef's recommendation?
- I wonder what the difference is between this and that.
- Which wine goes best with the dish?
- I'll have the same.
- What kind of dressing would you like?
- I didn't get my food yet.
- If it takes any longer, I'd like to cancel my order. I'm in a rush.
- There is a bug in my food. Could you please exchange it?

Lounge/ Bar

Jennifer: What would you like, sir?

Bill: I'd like a cognac, Remy Martin, if you have it.

Jennifer: Yes, we have it.

Bill: Give me scotch.

Jennifer: What brand?

Bill: White Horse, a double.

Chapter 7

Escort: Carring a Firearm

Firearms

There must be no doubt, when a security officer is carrying a firearm he or she is charged with the gravest of responsibilities. Let there be no doubt about this either, firearms were not devised as sporting equipment or for display purposes THEY WERE DESIGNED TO KILL!

Whilst there is a great deal of legislation in relation to the carriage and use of firearms, there is really only one basic paragraph that needs to be applied when answering any question of jurisdiction of the use of a firearm by a security guard.

"You may only use your firearm as a last resort, when you genuinely believe that your life, or the life of another person, is in grave and immediate danger, and there remains no other means by which you can protect yourself."

SAFE STORAGE OF FIREARMS

Under normal circumstances a security officer will leave his or her firearm under lock and key at their place of work during which times the employer is responsible for their safe and safe keeping.

On occasion however it may be impractical to return your firearm to your employer store of weapons at the end of your period of duty.

A security officer must undertaken in connection with the application of a license the officer must also undertake, at least once a year, further approved firearms safety training.

What do you do?

Jennifer: Are you Bill Jennings?

Bill: Yes, I am.

Are you Jennifer Nicholson?

Jennifer: That's right.

What do you do now, Bill?

Bill: I'm a student.

Jennifer: What are you studying?

Bill: I'm studying Hotel Management.

What do you do?

Jennifer: I'm a teacher in a college.

Bill: That's great.

When do you work?

Sally: Do you work in a bank?

Mark: Yes, I do. I'm a teller.

Sally: When do you work?

Mark: I work Monday through Friday.

Sally: Does your brother work in a fire station?

Mark: Yes, he does. He's a firefighter.

Sally: When does he work?

Mark: He leaves home 8:00 a.m. and gets back at 7:00 p.m.

What do these people do?

Pilot

Musician

Designer

Police officer

Teller

Teacher

Hairdresser

Computer programmer

Carpenter

Cook

Truck driver

Secretary

Farmer

Plumber

Clerk

repairman

Interview

* Choose an occupation.

* Decide where and when you will work.

* Write your information in the box.

Name	Simon	You	Your partner
Job	Policeman		
Leave home	8:00a.m.		
Transportation	Bus		
Work hours	9:00a.m. – 6:00p.m.		
Work place	Police station		
Transportation	Bus		
Get home	7:00p.m.		

Occupations

Actor
Actress
Baker
Chef
Construction worker
Dancer
Mechanic
Salesperson
Secretary
Singer
Superintendent
Teacher
Truck driver
Farmer
Firefighter
Policeman
Designer
Hairdresser
Pilot
Musician
Teller
Carpenter
Plumber
Repairman

Are you working?

Donald: Are you working?

Kevin: No, I'm not. I'm looking for a part-time job. Are you working?

Donald: No, I'm not.

Kevin: Why?

Donald: Because I want to learn English.

Kevin: Oh, I understand.

Donald: Is he working?

Kevin: No, he isn't. He isn't working.

Donald: Is he looking for a job?

Kevin: Yes, he is. He is looking for a job.

Donald: Does he want full-time or part-time job?

Kevin: He wants to work full-time.

Where do you work?

Judy: Where do you work?

Gary: I work in an office.

Judy: What do you do there?

Gary: I'm a secretary.

Judy: Where does your sister work?

Gary: She works in a police station.

Judy: What does she do?

Gary: She's a policewoman.

Who's Kevin?

Kevin is a student now. He was a salesman in Mexico. Kevin goes to school everyday. He studies English. He wants to be a kindergarten teacher.

Job Application

Last Name__________ First Name __________

Address ____________________

Telephone __________ Date of Birth __________

SEX male ☐ female ☐

Do you want full time? ☐ part time? ☐

What was your job? ____________________

How long at this job? ____________________

Signature ____________________

Date __________

Write the answers.

1. Who's a student?
2. Who was a salesman?
3. Where is Kevin from?
4. What was his job?
5. What's his job now?
6. Is he a fisherman?
7. Is he a student?
8. Is he a kindergarten teacher?

Chapter 8

Safety of Persons

Safety of Persons

The objective of providing close personal protection is to keep alive and well the person to whom the security officers are assigned to protect.

Successful provision for safety or persons requires the application of principles and procedures to daily life to minimize the risk of assassinations and kidnapping. Principal protection is possibly the most man-power intensive and costly form of Close Personal Protection.

VIP's and other persons in many and varied social and financial positions require Close Personal Protection. The reasons vary from Principal to Principal. A Rock and Roll Star requires protection from adoring fans who do not want to harm the Principal but never the less they require protection. A business man who is involved in a hostile take-over bid may require protection from either irate employee's or the other interested parties. Kidnapping may be another cause for Close Personal Protection.

Basic Conversation

Express Gratitude

- Thank you (very much). Thanks a lot.

  I appreciate what you've done.

- You're welcome.

  My pleasure.

  Not at all.

  Don't mention it.

Plead

- May I ask you a favor?
- Can you do it for me? Would you do something for me?
- Would you speak more slowly? Please speak more slowly.

Asking

- What is this?
- Can you speak English?
- Do you understand me?
- What's your name?

  May I ask your name?

  Could you spell your name for me?
- What time is it now? Do you have the time?

  Could you please tell me the time?

  What time do you have?
- How long does it take to the airport?
- What date is it today? What is the date today?
- What day of the week is today?

Apologize

- Excuse me.
- Pardon me.
- I am sorry.
- That's all right.
- That's OK.

Ask to Repeat

- I beg your pardon. Excuse me.

Suggestions Proposals

- How about this one? How about that one?
- How about going there with me?
- Shall we go? It's time to go. It's time for us to go.

Asking for Consideration or Understanding

- May I smoke? Is smoking allowed?
- May I open the window?
- Can I sit here? Is this seat taken?
- Just a moment, please.
  Wait a second, please.
  Hold on, please.
- Would you mind if I go out?

Introductions

Jennifer: Where are you from?
Bill: I'm from Korea.
Jennifer: How old are you?
Bill: I'm 35 years old.
Jennifer: This is my friend, Mr. Kim.
Bill: Glad to meet you, Mr. Kim.
Tom: Call me Tom.
Bill: Okay. Tom.

Pleasantries

- Nice day, isn't it?
- Lovely weather, isn't it?
- It's cold (hot), isn't it?
- It's raining outside.
- What's the temperature?
  What's the weather like?

What do you like to do?

Jennifer: Do you like Korean food?

Bill: Yes, I love it. What kind of food do you like?

Jennifer: I like Mexican food. Do you like Mexican food?

Bill: No, I don't. Do you like to cook?

Jennifer: Yes, I love cooking. It's my favorite hobby.

Bill: Well, I prefer watching TV.

Jennifer: Really? What kind of TV programs do you like?

Bill: I really like comedies.

Do you like these things?

Ask your partner if she/ he likes the same things.

Do you like it?

I like it.	*I don't like it.*
I like it very much.	*I dislike it.*
I love it.	*I hate it.*

1

2

3

4

5

6

Who's your favorite actor?

Bob: Do you like movies?

Susan: Not really. Do you?

Bob: Yes, especially action movies.

Susan: Who's your favorite actor?

Bob: My favorite actor is Tom Cruise. He's terrific. How about you?

Susan: I think Leonardo DiCaprio is a terrific actor. Who's your favorite actress?

Bob: I think Meg Ryan is terrific.

Guess the story.

Play this activity with in pairs or groups.

To play:

1. Make twenty cards showing a variety of people, places and things.
2. Stick picture cards on the wall or blackboard.
3. Prepare a story that includes five of the pictures.
4. Show which five pictures are used.
5. Don't say what the story is or in which order the four pictures come.
6. Tell the students they have to ask ten yes/no questions to find the story.
7. Encourage the students ask questions like these according to pictures.
8. Get the students to make up their own stories using five pictures.
9. Put them in pairs to guess each other's stories.
10. Announce the best story guesser.

(Sample yes/no questions)

- Do they like their job?
- Do they like to dance?
- Do they ever work overtime?
- Do they work on the weekend?
- Do they like to sing in a choir?
- Are they married or single?
- Does he like to play a basketball?

Chapter 9

Advance Security

Advance Security

At the Conference

Jennifer: What is the level of your country's security for the upcoming visit of the Korean President?

Bill: As the visit if your country's president to our country is an official visit, we plan to assume the highest level of security.

Jennifer: What is the size of Security Guard?

Bill: It's more than 100.

Jennifer: Who will be the doorman for the VIP car?

Bill: The Deputy Director of Detail Protection Division will be responsible for that.

Jennifer: What are the security measures during movement?

Bill: We will use a SWAT team at the rear of the motorcade.

Jennifer: What are the expected areas of (welcoming) crowds?

Bill: In front of the plaza.

Official visit
공식방문
The highest level of security
최고수준의 경호
Deputy Director
수행과장
During movement
기동간
SWAT
기동타격대

Jennifer: Where is the designated nearest hospital?

Bill: It's the Medical Center.

Jennifer: Who are the welcoming and line up members?

Bill: They are Korean residents (in U.S.A).

Jennifer: What are the security measures for the hotel guests?

Bill: Four uniformed police officers will rotate on two shifts.

Jennifer: Is this man one of your duty members?

Bill: Yes, he is.

Jennifer: How can I contact you?

Bill: Please, call to our CP.

Jennifer: I'd like to know about the operation of your security headquarters.

Bill: It will be set up two hours before the event, and will be located in a room on the hotel's twelfth floor.

Welcoming and line up members
영접인사와 도열인사

Uniformed police officers
정복경찰

two shifts
2교대근무

Security headquarters
경호본부

Jennifer: How are the emergency shelters?

Bill: We plan to use the basement of this hotel as the emergency shelter.

Jennifer: Will there be an ambulance standing by?

Bill: Yes, It will be in the parking lot behind the hotel.

Jennifer: How will we be able to distinguish your people?

Bill: Armed agents will be wearing this badge.

Jennifer: Here's a sample of our security badge. Now then, can you show us yours?

Bill: You can check directly with the agent in charge prior to the event for more detailed information.

Armed agents
총기소지경호원
Emergency shelters
비상대피소
Security badge
경호비표

Jennifer: Will there be press control?

Bill: Points for getting in and out of vehicles will be roped off, and in case of close-up photography, the press agent will be thoroughly regulated.

Press control
보도통제
Press agent
보도담당경호관
Close-up Photography
근거리촬영

Jennifer: Can you tell us something about the use of magnetometers?

Bill: We will use three of them, one at the front entrance, back entrance and the reception area.

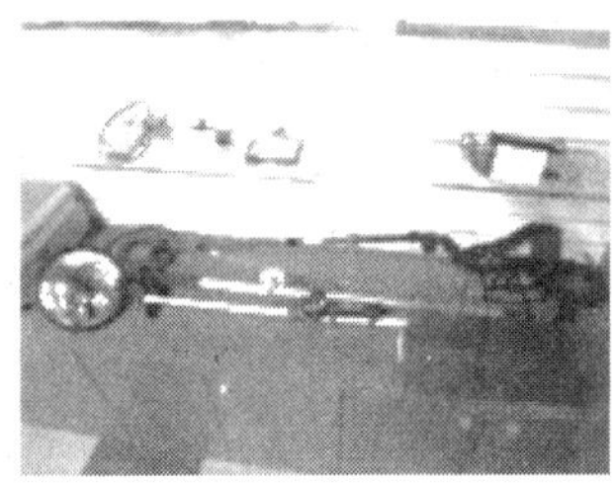

(Extension)

- I'm the officer-in-charge for the advance (attendance) party.
- I'm very glad to meet you.
- Here is my name card.
- Get me a city map.
- Get me a sketch of the activity site.
- Have a car stand-by all the time.
- I have a few questions, if you don't mind.

Advance Security

Security Responsibility

Jennifer: Who is in charge for the security guard?

Bill: We will be responsible for security, and through close mutual cooperation with your personnel, we will seek to provide the tightest security possible.

Jennifer: Please inform us as to the formation of a special security team and the time of its formation.

Bill: In preparation for the visit of your country's President and First Lady, we have set up a detailed plan for putting together a personal security team from D-7.

Close mutual cooperation
상호긴밀협조
The tightest security
완벽경호조치
Formation
편성

Jennifer: We request a chart of organization of your security team by specific duties, so that we may refer to it (while working)?

Bill: Please refer to this chart, as it contains a detailed description of the formation of our security team.

Jennifer: Which departments will be put in charge of security at each event site?

Bill: Secret service advance teams and each local police will be in charge of site security.

I'm calling from British Columbia.

Jennifer: Hi, Bill. This is Jennifer. I'm calling from British Columbia.

Bill: From British Columbia? What are you doing in British Columbia?

Jennifer: I'm on vacation.

Bill: How's the weather in British Columbia? Is it cool?

Jennifer: No, it isn't. It's windy.

Bill: Is it hot?

Jennifer: No, it isn't. It's cold.

What city are you from?

Jennifer: What city are you from?

Bill: I am from Montreal.

Jennifer: Where is Montreal?

Bill: It is in Canada.

Brasilia
Cape Town
San Antonio
Sydney
St. Petersburg
Bangkok
Seoul
Bruges
Montreal
Irapuato
Guiyang
Ho Chi Minh
London
Canberra
Paris
Beijing
Osaka

What is Lucy doing tomorrow?

Ask your partner questions and fill in the missing information.

Lucy is getting up at 8:00 a.m.

She's eating breakfast ______.

She's leaving home at 8:45.

She's getting to school at ______.

She's having lunch at noon.

She's going to the gym at ______.

Lucy is getting up at ______.

She's eating breakfast at 8:15.

She's leaving home at ______.

She's getting to school at 10:00.

She's having lunch ______.

She's going to the gym at 5:00 p.m.

Chapter 10

Advance Security
Site Security

Advance Security

Indoor, outdoor

Jennifer: Please let us know about your advance security plans and any combined activities with our people.

Combined activities
합동경호활동
Entrance screening
출입통제
Personnel
요원

Bill: Our advance contingent security consists of technical search and securing of event sites from H-2 carried out by SS personnel, and if you desire, combined activities are possible.

Jennifer: Please inform us of plans for the entrance securing of participants to the sites.

Bill: As the sites are to be guarded by combined forces, entrance screening shall be carried out after identification of your personnel by you and our personnel by us.

Jennifer: Please tell us when an advance team of ours might survey each site beforehand.

Bill: We will do everything possible to accommodate you in this area, but please understand that circumstances may not permit in some locations.

(Extension)

- Where is the Security Command Post?
- What is the guide course?
- I'd like to have a copy of the duty roster.
- How many and where are the duty posts?
- Where is the VIP room?
- I'd like to have the master key to the VIP room.
- Show me the floor plan of the building.
- Set the elevator on "Non-stop".
- This is a restricted area.
- What can I do for you?
- I'll check and take care of it.
- Show your personal belongings, please.
- Step back a little, please.
- Go the other way around, please.
- Are the workers (hotel guests) cleared?
- Block that side.
- What is the closing time for guests?
- Is there any change on the guide course?
- Unload the gun, please.
- Where is the hydrant?
- Are the fire-proof jackets ready?
- Are the oxygen gas masks ready?
- What is the emergency power transfer plan?

Security Command Post
경호지휘부
Guide course
안내코스
Duty roster
근무편성표
Duty Post
근무초소
Restricted area
통제구역
Personal belongings
개인소지품
Unload the gun
실탄제거
Fire-proof
방열복
Hydrant
소화전

Security Badges

Jennifer: Please describe plans for the use of badges.

Bill: We will provide badges for our agents to power, and would appreciate if your people would wear the same badges.

Jennifer: Will there be any additional badges provided for our personnel who will need to have access to the guest quarters or other restricted areas?

Bill: We plan to issue access passes to necessary personnel.

Guest quarter
영빈관
Necessary personnel
필수요원

Emergency Countermeasures

Jennifer: It would be much help to us if you could inform us about the proposed closest hospitals to each site and about their current status.

Bill: We have arranged for essential personnel to be on stand-by and have selected the closest hospitals for each site in case of emergency. The status of each site is contained in this memo.

Jennifer: It would be helpful if you could inform us about your security command post operation and location.

Bill: Our command post will be on the first floor of the guest quarters (next to yours), and we suggest utilizing someone as a liaison in order for both sides to keep in close communication.

Jennifer: Please inform us of emergency helicopters, and routes in case of fire or other emergencies in the hotel.

Bill: Please refer to the basic security plan we have provided for that kind of information.

Press Control

Jennifer: Please tell us of plans for controlling the press corps.

Bill: Both our countries should as a rule screen our respective press members and those who refuse to comply we plan to bar from coverage activities.

May I help you?

Bill: May I help you?

Jennifer: I'm looking for a watch for my father.

Bill: Well, we have several very nice watches here.

Jennifer: How much is that gold watch on the right?

Bill: It's $525.00

Jennifer: Oh, it's very nice, but it's too expensive.

Bill: Well, how about this one on the left? It's only $150.00

Jennifer: Yes, I like that one. And I think I can afford it. I'll take it.

Write a flyer for the store.

* Draw clothes in your flyer.
* Your store is having a sale.
* Put the prices, hours, phone number, location map, and the name of the store.
* Present your flyer in the class.

Can I help you find something?

Fred: Can I help you find something?

Lisa: Yes, I'm looking for some tennis shoes.

Fred: These blue and white Nikes are 30% off.

Lisa: I don't like the color.

Fred: Then how about these Reebok shoes?

Lisa: How much are they?

Fred: They are $89.95 a pair.

Lisa: Oh, I can't afford that.

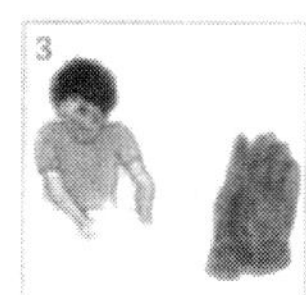

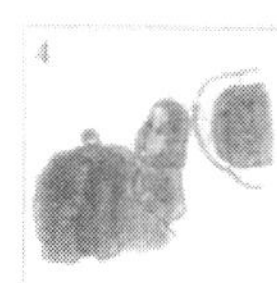

~~~~~~~~~~~~~~~~~~~~~~~~~~~~~~~~

LOOKING FOR A PRESENT

* Work with a partner.
* One of you is a sales clerk and the other is looking for one of these presents for the relatives or friends shown.

~~~~~~~~~~~~~~~~~~~~~~~~~~~~~~~~

How much is it?

Judy: I like this dress. How much is it?

Gary: Now it's $25.00 on sale.

Judy: On sale?

Gary: Yes, it was $35.00.

Judy: I'll take it. How much are these socks?

Gary: They are four dollars a pair. How many pairs do you need?

Judy: I need three pairs.

Gary: That will be twelve dollars, please.

On Sale

Sweaters $7.99 each, reg. $9.00. Many colors and styles. Women's S-M-L Cotton-polyester knit.

1. What's on sale?
2. What colors can you buy?
3. What sizes can you buy?
4. What are they made of?
5. What's the regular price?
6. What's the sale price?
7. How much can you save?

Chapter 11

Security at the Airport

Security at the Airport

Jennifer: When do you expect the VIP's plane?

Bill: It will arrive at 9 p.m.

Jennifer: Which runway will be used?

Bill: That plane will stop at gate 13 by way of main runway.

Jennifer: Where is the VIP lounge?

Bill: It's on the 2nd floor of this building.

Jennifer: Who are the welcome parties?

Bill: He's the Foreign Minister.

Jennifer: Who is the officer-in-charge of protocol?

Bill: A protocol secretary.

Jennifer: What kind of weapon do you carry?

Bill: It's a 38-caliber revolver.

Jennifer: What is the duty shift plan?

Bill: We will work in three shifts of six hours.

Jennifer: How many airport security guards are there?

Bill: Four agents.

Jennifer: What is the location of the officer-in-charge for the airport security?

Bill: He is in the office of airport security guards.

Jennifer: When and where do you check the cargo?

Bill: We will check into a hotel tonight.

Jennifer: Where is the gas station?

Bill: You can fill up at the designated gas station.

Jennifer: How long does it take to fill up?

Bill: It takes 10 minutes.

Jennifer: Who is the officer-in-charge of gasoline?

Bill: He is in charge of our special aircraft security.

Jennifer: Will the gun salute be offered in this case?

Bill: It will not be offered in this case.

Jennifer: What kind of facilities can we use at the airport?

Bill: If necessary, you can use all ground facilities.

(Extension)

- Set the rear trap first, please.
- Show me the plan for the activities, please.
- Have you checked the press and their equipment?
- What is the control plan for welcoming crowds?
- Is the trap ready?
- Be careful when you load the cargo.
- Load VIP cargo here.
- What do you think about the vulnerability of this airway?
- Show me the layout of the airport.

Advance Security

Special Aircraft Security

Jennifer: Would you briefly describe your plans for guarding the special aircraft?

Bill: Base security is in charge of that, and the aircraft is roped off while on the ground to prevent access.

Jennifer: How do you use the security forces?

Bill: Two men are on duty for two hours at a time, and one patrol car will be placed next to the plane.

Jennifer: Where will the aircraft be waiting?

Bill: It will be moved to its waiting area after the welcoming ceremony.

Jennifer: Is there a place for our personnel to wait while on duty? And, it would be great if I have a phone to be able to contact off-post.

Bill: Yes. Use the office across the way. You can see the aircraft waiting area from there, and it also has a phone you can use.

Jennifer: Is there anything in particular prepared for special aircraft security?

Bill: At night, 3 lights will be installed along the perimeter.

Jennifer: Where is the weather station?

Bill: On the second floor of this building. If you need weather forecasts, you can request them from there.

Matching Useful Expressions.

A. Listen and repeat the Jennifer's expressions.

1. Jennifer: How can I get downtown?
2. Jennifer: What bus number goes downtown?
3. Jennifer: How much is the bus fare?
4. Jennifer: Where can I catch the bus?
5. Jennifer: What time does the bus leave?
6. Jennifer: Where is the subway?

B. Choose and match the questions from part A in the blank spaces.

1. Jennifer: ____________________
   Bill: You can get on the bus across the street.
2. Jennifer: ____________________
   Bill: The 349 bus goes downtown.
3. Jennifer: ____________________
   Bill: The subway is beside McDonalds.
4. Jennifer: ____________________
   Bill: You can take a bus downtown.
5. Jennifer: ____________________
   Bill: It leaves every 10 minutes.
6. Jennifer: ____________________
   Bill: It's $3.00.

Practice the dialogue.

Practice the following dialogue with your partner. Use the information below in the blank spaces.

Jennifer: Where are you going for your vacation?

Bill: I'm going to ________________.

Jennifer: When are you going?

Bill: I'm leaving on ______________.

Jennifer: Really! When will you come back?

Bill: I arrive in Korea on ___________.

Jennifer: Sounds like fun. How much is the fare?

Bill: The fare is _________________.

Jennifer: That's not bad. I wish I could go.

Destination	Departure date	Arrival date	Fare
Tokyo	August 10	August 24	$500.00
Vancouver	July 20	August 4	$900.00
Paris	September 5	September 19	$1,200.00
Cairo	October 1	October 15	$1,300.00
Melbourne	November 7	November 21	$800.00
London	December 12	December 25	$1,400.00

What time does the bus come?

Jennifer: Hello, Bus Company.

Bill: Hello, I'm on Jefferson Street.

Jennifer: Where are you going?

Bill: I'm going downtown.

Jennifer: Are you taking the bus?

Bill: Yes, I am. What bus goes downtown?

Jennifer: Take the 1001 bus.

Bill: Do I need transfer?

Jennifer: No, you don't.

Bill: What time does the bus come?

Jennifer: Every hour.

Bill: Thank you. Bye.

Jennifer: Bye.

Can you tell me how to get to your house?

Jennifer: Can you tell me how to get to your house?

Bill: Sure. Go straight to the 1st Street three blocks. Turn right on Spring Avenue. Go two blocks. Turn left on the 2nd Street. Go one block.

Jennifer: What's your address?

Bill: It's 779 Second Street.

Jennifer: How long does it take to get there?

Bill: It takes about twenty minutes.

Give the direction using useful expressions

Get to
Turn right
Turn left
Take a left turn
Take a right turn
Walk up
Walk down
Walk cross
Walk along
Right around the corner
On the left
On the right
Go straight
Across from
Opposite from
Next to
Between
Around the corner from
In front of

Security English

Chapter 12

Air Trip

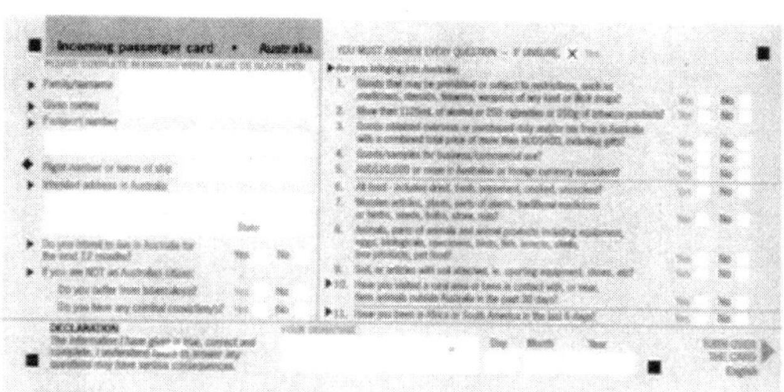
Incoming passenger card • Australia

DECLARATION

Air Trip Reservations

Jennifer: I'd like to book a flight to New York. I'd like to make a reservation to New York.

Do you have a direct (non-stop) flight?

Bill: It flies to New York via Anchorage.

We have one leaving at 7.

There's one leaving at 7.

Air Trip Fares.

Jennifer: How much does it cost to fly to LA?

What is the fare to LA?

How much is it for round-trip ticket from Seoul to Paris?

Do you have any lower (cheaper) fares?

Is this ticket refundable?

Is this ticket transferable?

Air Travel Time

Jennifer: How many hours does the flight take? How long is the flight?
What are the departure and arrival time?
What's the flight time from here to London?

Air Trip Boarding

Jennifer: Would you show me your boarding pass, please?

Bill: Here it is.

Jennifer: Your seat number is 25A. It is over there by the (right side/ left side) window.

Bill: Thank you.

Tony: Excuse me, my seat number is 12D. Where is it?

Jennifer: It is right over there on the aisle.

Air Trip Cabin Service

Jennifer: Would you like a newspaper?

May I get you a newspaper?

Can I bring you something to drink?

Would you care for something to drink?

Bill: Will you show me a brochure for duty-free items?

May I see a duty-free brochure?

Please don't wake me up.

Please don't disturb me.

Air Trip Cabin Shopping

Jennifer: I'd like to buy cigarettes. Do you have Marlboro Light.

Bill: Yes, we have. How many cartons would you like?

Jennifer: Two cartons, please. How much do I owe you (How much is that)?

Bill: Eighteen dollars, sir.

Jennifer: Can I pay in Korean currency

Bill: Yes, of course.
O. K. Sure.
By all means.

Air Trip Take off

Announcement

Flight 011 is now leaving for Los Angeles via Honolulu. Please, put your seat in the upright position and fasten your seat belt until the sign is turned off. Thank you.

Air Trip Delay

Announcement

I'm very sorry to inform you that Flight 011 is behind schedule due to bad weather conditions. Please be seated as we are going to take off as soon as the weather clears. Thank you.

Air Trip Landing Announcement

We have just landed at Los Angeles International Airport. The local time here in Los Angeles is 1:30 p. m. The weather here is cloudy and the temperature is currently 65 degrees Fahrenheit. Please be sure to take all of your belongings when you leave the plane. We hope you have enjoyed the flight and may have the opportunity to serve you again in the near future. Thank you.

Practical Conversations

Duty-Free Shop

Jennifer: This is a duty-free shop, isn't it?

Bill: Yes, but only on the first floor.

Jennifer: I'd like to buy some brandy.

Bill: May I see your passport?
Fine. Which brand do you want?

Jennifer: One of those and one of these.

Bill: Would you like to buy some perfume, too?

INCOMING PASSENGER CARD

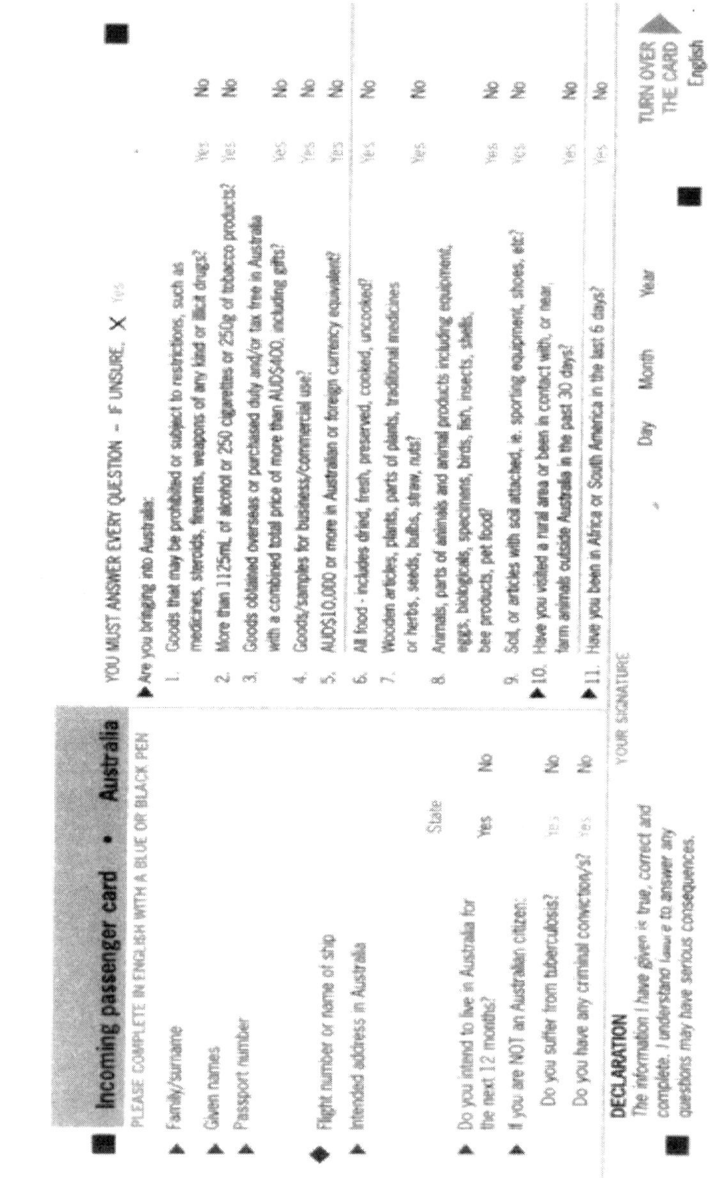

Incoming passenger card • Australia

PLEASE COMPLETE IN ENGLISH WITH A BLUE OR BLACK PEN

- Family/surname
- Given names
- Passport number
- Flight number or name of ship
- Intended address in Australia

State

- Do you intend to live in Australia for the next 12 months? Yes No
- If you are NOT an Australian citizen:
  - Do you suffer from tuberculosis? Yes No
  - Do you have any criminal conviction/s? Yes No

YOU MUST ANSWER EVERY QUESTION – IF UNSURE, X Yes

Are you bringing into Australia:

1. Goods that may be prohibited or subject to restrictions, such as medicines, steroids, firearms, weapons of any kind or illicit drugs? Yes No
2. More than 1125mL of alcohol or 250 cigarettes or 250g of tobacco products? Yes No
3. Goods obtained overseas or purchased duty and/or tax free in Australia with a combined total price of more than AUD$400, including gifts? Yes No
4. Goods/samples for business/commercial use? Yes No
5. AUD$10,000 or more in Australian or foreign currency equivalent? Yes No
6. All food - includes dried, fresh, preserved, cooked, uncooked? Yes No
7. Wooden articles, plants, parts of plants, traditional medicines or herbs, seeds, bulbs, straw, nuts? Yes No
8. Animals, parts of animals and animal products including equipment, eggs, biologicals, specimens, birds, fish, insects, shells, bee products, pet food? Yes No
9. Soil, or articles with soil attached, ie. sporting equipment, shoes, etc? Yes No
10. Have you visited a rural area or been in contact with, or near, farm animals outside Australia in the past 30 days? Yes No
11. Have you been in Africa or South America in the last 6 days? Yes No

DECLARATION

The information I have given is true, correct and complete. I understand failure to answer any questions may have serious consequences.

YOUR SIGNATURE

Day Month Year

TURN OVER THE CARD

English

PLEASE COMPLETE IN ENGLISH

▶ In which country did you board this flight or ship?

◆ What is your usual occupation?

▶ Nationality as shown on passport

▶ Date of birth   Day   Month   Year

▶ PLEASE X AND ANSWER A OR B OR C

A Migrating permanently to Australia

B Visitor or temporary entrant

▶ Your intended length of stay in Australia   Years   Months   OR   Days

▶ Your country of residence

▶ Your main reason for coming to Australia (X one only)

Convention/conference	1	Employment	4	Holiday	7
Business	2	Education	5	Other	8
Visiting friends or relatives	3	Exhibition	6		

C Resident returning to Australia

▶ Country where you spent most time abroad

MAKE SURE YOU HAVE COMPLETED BOTH SIDES OF THIS CARD. PRESENT THIS CARD ON ARRIVAL WITH YOUR PASSPORT.

Information sought on this form is required to administer immigration, customs, quarantine, statistical, health, wildlife and currency laws of Australia and its collection is authorised by legislation. It will be disclosed only to agencies administering these areas and those entitled to receive it under Australian law. The leaflet *Safeguarding your personal information* is available at Australian ports and airports.

07021505

15 (Design date 07/02)

McMILLAN PRINT

Chapter 13

Control Crowds

Control Crowds

Any security officer might find themselves in a crowd control situation, be it a retail officer who suddenly has to control crowds due to unscheduled in store appearance of a sporting celebrity or a fully briefed crowd control team member at the Easter Show.

The three main areas in which crowd controllers are generally required are sporting or large-scale events, rock or musical concerts, and hotels, club and pubs.

Crowd Control
군중통제
Sporting Celebrity
스포츠유명인사
Easter Show
부활축제

The Duties of a Crowd Controller

No matter what crowd control situation we find ourselves in, we have certain rcsponsibilities and duties as crowd controllers.

Crowd controllers ensure that all staff and patrons are provided with a safe environment, all persons attending the event, function, premises etc. behave in an acceptable and responsible manner, and all persons adhere to venue specific codes of conduct and all legal requirements are adhered to.

They should ensure the safety of fellow work colleagues and be observant of crowd behavior and investigate and resolve potential or identified problems within the crowd.

They ensure that all entry and exit procedures are followed and the smooth entry and egress from venues or premises.

Patron
고객
Venue
현장
Fellow Work Colleagues
현장동료
Entry and Egress
출입구

Relationship with Clients

There are many factors to be considered when looking to present the right image. Not only is clothing (uniform, plain clothes) a factor, but so are grooming, posture, general demeanor and even the type of body language being projected.

General Demeanor
품행
Uniform Appearance
정복차림

A client will make selections based on the same criteria, so presenting a uniform appearance is an excellent starting point for good client relations. The client will invariably try and communicate to you type of service or product they wish to obtain. You can best facilitate this process by performing listening, questioning and summarizing.

Security Work

The nature of security work makes it vitally important for all security officers to understand the concept of teamwork, how a security team should function, understanding individual roles within a team environment, the provision of individual and team back up procedures, team briefings and debriefing sessions and working as part of a team or leading a team.

Team Back Up
팀지원
Team Briefings
팀결과보고
Debriefing Sessions
결과보고듣기

Teamwork is about understanding and respecting the other members of the team. It's about effective communication of tasks and effective leadership to complete those tasks to the required standard. Good teamwork take time to develop and the longer a group of security officers spend together the better the team spirit and focus between them.

Intelligence

Jennifer: Please tell me of intelligence regarding VIP attack, related to the visit of our president.

Bill: We haven't any intelligence on VIP attack so far, but an anti-government demonstration will be held around the site.

Jennifer: Is there anything special related to this visit regarding recent movements of N.K. officials and residents.

Bill: Even though we don't know of any unusual behavior yet, we are investigating movements of North Korean.

Jennifer: Could you explain about the general security of the city briefly? And please confirm whether areas with bad security situation are.

Bill: Security in this area is relatively good, but some drug and violent crimes happen as they do in other metropolitan cities. However, there isn't a problem protecting VIPs.

Anti-Government Demonstration
반정부시위

Drug and Violent Crimes
마약폭력범죄

Preliminary Threat Reports
사전위협보고

Jennifer: Which division is in charge of collecting and handling security intelligence and information?

Bill: We have several intelligence services, and secret service is receiving security intelligence from them.

Jennifer: Do your agents stand by in C.P. and are they going out to the site during the event?

Bill: Sure, we will. Whenever we get security intelligence, we will send it to you.

Jennifer: Please tell us whether there are arrangements for back-up guards at sites about where there are preliminary threat reports.

Bill: We have prior arrangement for the immediate back-up by area police at sites for which there is perceived danger according to analysis of such information.

Practical Conversations

Shopping

- Can I have it gift-wrapped?
- Can I have it delivered?
- Can I have them shipped to Korea?
- What are some special products of this town?
- Please send it by air.
- Isn't there a mistake in the bill?
- Can I change this?
- Please show me the one in the window.

At the Post Office

Jennifer: Hi. I need two aerogram and a post card, please.

Bill: Here you are. That will be $4.50.

Jennifer: I'd like this mail registered.

Bill: All right. It is 5 dollars and 35 cents. Please fill out this form.

Jennifer: Here's 5 dollars and 35 cents.

Bill: Thank you. I'll give you a receipt.

(Extension)

- I'd like to send this letter (postcard) by air (sea) mail.
- How long will it take to reach Korea?
- I'd like to buy a money order for $100.00
- Please register this letter (parcel).

Phone Calls

- Would someone answer the phone?
- Who's calling, please?
- I just called a minute ago.
- Speaking. It's me.
- It's for you.
- We have a bad connection.
- Would you mind repeating it?
- I'm afraid you have the wrong number.
- There's no one here by that name.
- What is this call regarding?
- That's all I have to tell you.
- Please give my regards to your family.
- Please put me through to extension 2103.
  Extension 2103, please.
- I'm sorry, but his line is busy at the moment.
- Would you hold for a moment? Please hold.

Judy's Answering Machine

Hi, there. You have reached 850-1298. This is Judy Smith. I'm sorry I can't come to the phone right now, but if you leave your name and number after beep, I'll get back to you as soon as possible. Thank you. Bye. (Beep)

- Shall I take a message?
- I'm expecting a call. So please take a message for me while I'm gone.
- He's on a business trip now.
- How can I get in touch with you?
- Please leave your message on the answering machine if I'm not home.
- I'd like place an international call to Korea.
- Can you please connect me for a collect call? Collect call, please?
- We have an overseas collect call from Korea.

Gary's Incoming Message:
Judy, This is Gary Miller from the First National Bank, South City Branch. I'm calling to tell you that your application has been accepted.
Congratulations. Please call us back as soon as possible. Thank you. Good bye.

Security English

Chapter 14

Emergency

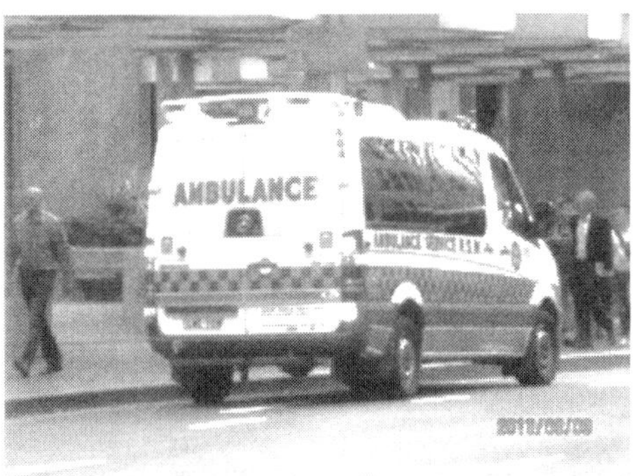

Emergency

Fire Safety

Bill: Today's detail is a check on fire safety procedures and a point check on required fire safety tools.

Jennifer: Yes, sir. The fire fighting team is here to go through it with us

Bill: Great. Is the stand by fire engine available?

Jennifer: No. Not today. But, it will be here on the day of operations.

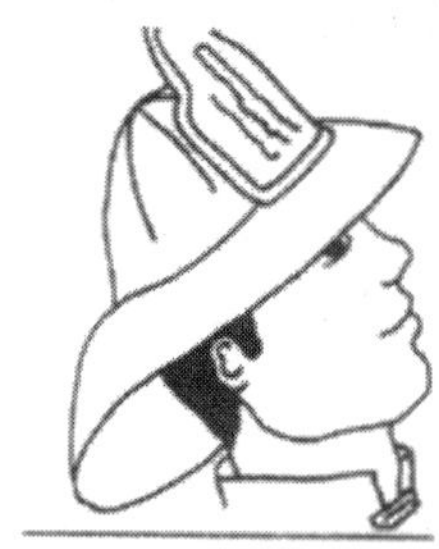

Bill: That's fine. First, let's check on the elevated ladders, pumps and chemical car.

Jennifer: Check.

Bill: Next, the inside and outside fire hydrant.

Jennifer: Check.

Bill: Are the fire extinguishers available inside the complex?

Jennifer: There are three of them at every exit.

Bill: We need fire proof jackets. Three of them.

Jennifer: Got them, sir. One for the president, the first lady and me.

Bill: For you?

Jennifer: Yes, sir. I will be carrying the presidential dog.

Fire Safety, Fire Extinguishers

Portable fire extinguishers can save lives and property by putting out or containing small fires. However, they must be of the correct type for the particular fire. They must also be used correctly and they must only be used on small fires.

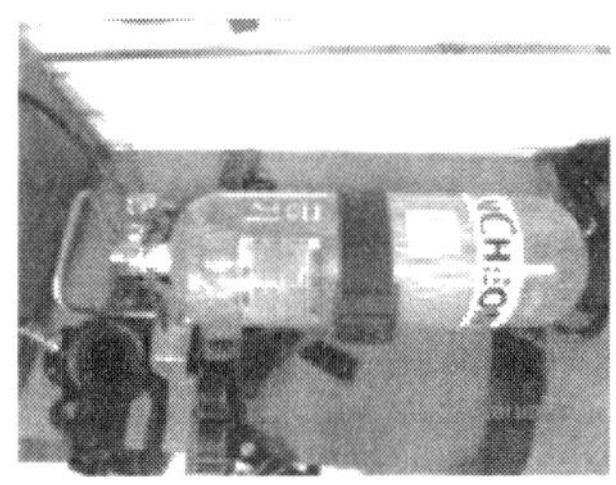

The most common types of extinguishers are water which are not considered effective on fires involving flammable liquids and gases, and dangerous if used on live electrical equipment or cooking oils or fats, foam which are not considered effective on fires involving flammable gases, and dangerous if used on live electrical equipment, and powder which are not considered effective on class F fires.

Emergency

Baggage Convoy

Jennifer: Are the rescue vehicles here?

Bill: Yes, they are.

Jennifer: How about the operations of the electricians and firemen? Who has the schedule?

Tony: That would be me ma'am.

Jennifer: Sam. Do you have the safety measures for firearms and explosives?

Sam: Yes. I also have the time of arrival at the hotel of the baggage convoy.

Jennifer: Great. Agent Two, Bill. Who will be at the gathering place of baggage?

Bill: That will be agent two, me.

Jennifer: Make sure the customs procedure of the baggage goes smoothly.

Bill: Yes, ma'am. Would you also like me to take charge of prior transportation of the VIP baggage?

Jennifer: No. Agent three, Sam will do that.

Sam: Yes, ma'am. I will also detail the emergency security measures.

Jennifer: Great. Now, where is that bomb dog? I think it took my lunch.

Emergency Evacuation

Security officers may be called upon in times of emergency to deal with and manage the various aspects of building evacuation procedures and safe maintenance of a clients or employers premises.

It is not the actual catastrophe (fire, bomb threat, toxic leak etc.) that caused the emergency situation that results in injuries to persons rather it is during the unguided panic stricken mass "*escape*" from building that people are injured.

Breaking crowds into smaller groups makes them easier to handle in an emergency situation!

Bomb Threat

Because bomb threat causes enormous disruption to commerce, the strategies need to be designed and implemented to assess the level of the threat and to establish whether or not evacuation should in fact take place.

Although the vast majority of bomb threats are in fact hoaxes, people are still adversely affected, productivity decreases, staff, police, and security personnel waste many man hours and it is impossible to measure the fear and apprehension people experience.

Most bomb threats are made on the telephone.

Emergency

Traffic Accident

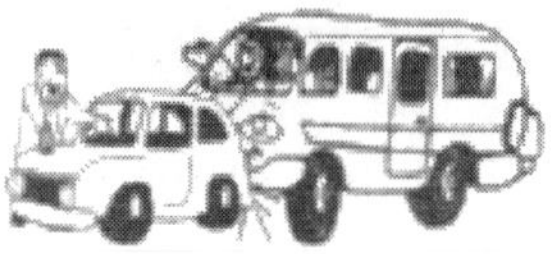

- Please help me!
- Please call an ambulance!
- He crossed the street against the traffic signal.
- He was jay-walking.
- The car ahead of me made a sudden stop.
- It wasn't my fault.
- Can I see your license and insurance policy (certificate)?
- I'll be careful from now on.

Robbery/ Lost Articles

- There's the pickpocket!
- Help! I got robbed!
- My bag was stolen. I had my passport, money, and some checks in it.
- I will fill out a theft report.
- Did he use a weapon?
- Please cancel my credit card.
- Would you contact the Korean Embassy for me, please?
- I left my camera in the bus.
- Where should I go to ask about lost articles?
- If you find it, please contact the number on this memo.

Emergency

Disease/ Sickness

- I'd like to see a doctor.
- Can I make an appointment to see Dr. Kim?
- This is an emergency. Please call a doctor.
- How much does he charge for each visit?
- Breathe in slowly.
- I've broken my leg.
- I've sprained my ankle.
- What do you think the problem is?
- How long will it take me to recover fully?
- Is it all right to drink alcohol?
- I'll prescribe some medicine for three days.
- Take this after each meal three times a day.
- These pills will help digestion.

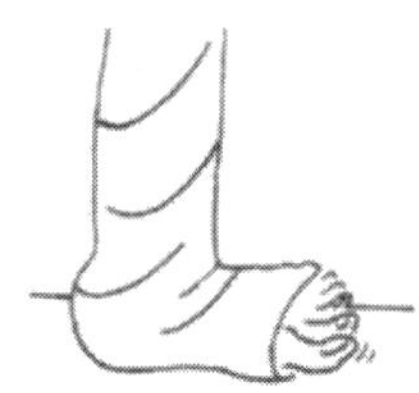

Medical Care

Jennifer: Where does ambulance stand by?
Bill: It is standing by at the site.
Jennifer: Where is the available hospital?
Bill: Most hospitals are available.
Jennifer: Will the ambulance stand by the residence during night?
Bill: Yes, I will order it.
Jennifer: What is the blood type of the VIP?
Bill: It is A positive.

Emergency Reporting Procedure

The accurate record and report of the incidents needs to be presented to your organization and to your clients. The method of recording information should be adopted: Always start a notebook entry off with *time, date and place* (ie. location of incidents), followed by *details of the incident* (ie. What was it about, what was damaged). During the course of the incident people will be spoken to in relation to it, so record the *details of any persons involved*, including witnesses and the *names, ranks, stations of any emergency services personnel* that you may have dealt with. And of course you must *record any action taken by you.*

The incident report will be required to complete an assignment response report *ISSUE, BACKGROUND, ACTION TAKEN,* and *RECOMMENDATION.*

Technical Detection

Jennifer: We will appreciate your informing us how to search at the sites.

Bill: Searches will be conducted at each site by a special technical security team, and their utilization time will be decided as per the nature and characteristics of the site.

Jennifer: Is there the possibility of combined search activities with our technical security team?

Bill: As a rule it is possible, but please be advised that it may be difficult to accommodate you in restricted areas.

Jennifer: We wish to know your methods of luggage detection.

Bill: We inspect all articles of luggage, outside of that of dignitaries, by means of X-ray and bomb dogs.

Jennifer: Please explain how VIP luggage will be transported and transport vehicles concerned.

Bill: A luggage van is to be provided by Secret Service, and one agent of ours will be accompanied by your security personnel during transport.

Jennifer: Please inform us of any plans for metal Detector operation to search the participants.

Bill: We will use three of them, one at the front entrance, back entrance and the reception area, and we will install them at seven tomorrow morning.

Jennifer: What are your plans for searches?

Bill: We will begin two hours before the event when security people are deployed and local police EOD teams and bomb dogs will assist our technical security teams.

Food Inspection

Jennifer: Please inform us as to the nature of VIP food and beverage inspection, and of the possibility of this being a joint activity.

Bill: We normally take care of all food inspection ourselves, but if you desire, we will gladly accommodate you by making it a cooperative activity.

Chapter 15

Transportation

Transportation

Road Information

Jennifer: Could you show me the way?

I don't know which way I should take.

Which way should I go?

Can you tell me how to get to the Hilton Hotel?

Bill: I'm going in the same direction.

I'm going that way.

Jennifer: Is it close to the hotel?

Bill: It's a five minute walk from the subway station.

Public Transportation

- Are there any other buses going there?
- What's the one-way (round trip) fare?
- I'd like to have a reserved seat ticket.
- How long is this ticket good for?
- At what station should I get off?
- Please tell me where I have to change trains.
- I missed my stop.
- I've been waiting for 20 minutes, but I still haven't gotten a cab.
- There's a taxi stand over there.
- Please hurry. I've got to be at the airport by six.
- Can you drop me in front of the hotel?
- Could you pick me up in an hour?

Car/ Automobile

- I'd like to buy a car.
- I'm looking for a used car.
- Can I take it for a trial run (test drive)?
- Do I have to buy both the accident and the liability coverage?
- What's the charge per hour?
- Fill it up, please.
- It's out of gas.
- Where is the spare tire?
- I'd like to wipe the windshield.
- Please charge the battery.
- The oil is leaking.
- I've locked myself out of the car.
- I've got a flat (tire).
- I'd like a gas saving car.

Car Hire and Rental

How do I make a booking?

You can book a car quick and easy by following the 3 easy steps. After selecting the dates and location, we will search for the cheapest price for your rental.

On the car selection page you can select the preferred car. If you wish to add options/ equipment to your booking you can click the "ADD OPTIONS" button. By selecting any option/ equipment, we will search again,

On the last page you will see the booking summary, please check again the dates to make sure that you booked the car for the correct dates. When you enter your personal details and press the "Book Now" button, an e-mail with your order number will be sent to you. As soon as one of our car rental providers confirms your booking, the voucher will be sent to you.

All details about the pickup will be mentioned on your voucher. All details about the pickup will be mentioned on your voucher.

All drivers need to present a valid driver's licence and the ID card/ Passport as well as a credit card issued on the driver's name.

Driving Downunder can drive you crazy

Allan Whiting reveals the cunning traps that await US visitors

AUSTRALIA MAGAZINE

Driving upside down is tricky. Aussies derive great amusement from watching American visitors struggling to come to terms with our left-hand side of the road, right-hand driving environment.

We got our right-hand drive concept from the British, where Americans got their tea.

The logic of right-hand drive dates back to the days when men rode horses and wore swords. If you were on the left hand side of a road or a bridle path you could draw your weapon and take guard or strike quite easily. If you were on the opposite side of the track you'd have to turn your horse around – unless you were left-handed, which was considered 'unsporting'.

We must therefore assume that the American who decided that US vehicles would be left-hand drive must have been left-handed.

Another legacy of the British is the national rail gauge in Australia – British Standard Gauge, or four feet eight and one-half inches. If that seems an odd dimension look back to the width of Roman chariot axles, which led to British wagon axles, which led to British rail axles. But I digress...

Even though we don't wear swords these days – in fact wearing any weapon in public is an offence in most Australian States – we still travel on the left-hand side of the road. That means the steering wheel is on the right-hand side of the car and the gear lever is on the left hand side of the wheel. It's funny watching an American trying to change gear by putting a right arm out the right-side driver's window.

Not so funny is watching American visitors stepping off the kerb, looking the wrong way for oncoming traffic! Street crossing is very dangerous until you get used to the opposite traffic flow. Trouble is, you just get used to it and then it's time to head back Stateside and re-learn what used to be a habit.

Hire car companies Downunder try to make the right-hand drive experience easier by putting "Keep Left" stickers on windscreens and sunvisors and most US visitors get the idea pretty quickly.

Turns are always interesting – particularly right-hand turns across oncoming traffic lanes into two-way streets. A right-hand turn in the USA is easy, but in Australia it's the equivalent of a US left-hand turn. It's difficult to overcome the feeling that you're going to be overtaken during the turn and it's problematic picking which side of the new street to head for.

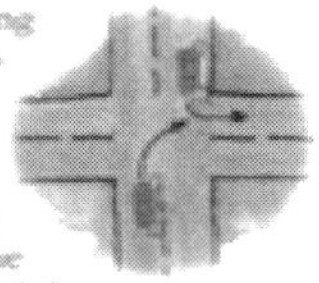

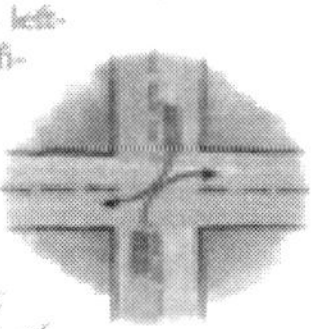

Another problem is that in the USA right hand turns – the equivalent of our left-hand turn – can be done at red lights after stopping the vehicle.

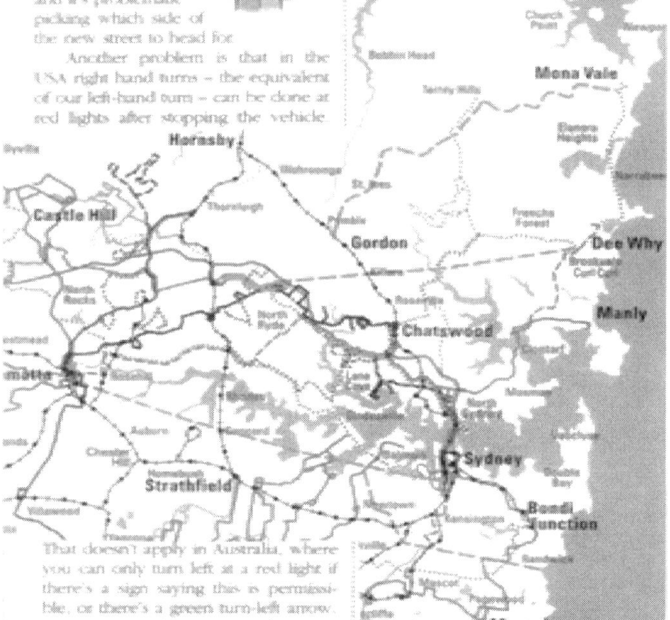

That doesn't apply in Australia, where you can only turn left at a red light if there's a sign saying this is permissible, or there's a green turn-left arrow.

Most US drivers soon feel pretty happy with their upside down driving efforts and don't realise how much they depend on the road lane markings for orientation.

On back roads, with no centre line, it's not quite so easy to keep left.

I remember one hilarious episode at an Outback roadhouse. I'd pulled up for fuel and tucker and was heading back onto the dirt road when an American-driven hire car entered the roadhouse driveway from the opposite direction.

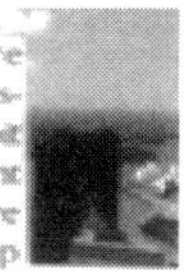

I steered left – as we do Downunder – and the visitor steered where his habit took him – to his right. I went more left and he went more right, until we finished up facing each other.

He just started to tell his wife how dopey we Aussies were, before it dawned on him that he'd steered the 'wrong' way. No damage was done and we all just cracked up.

Another headache for US drivers is Australia's metric system – when you see a speed limit sign that says '110' it doesn't mean you can drive at 110 miles an hour – unless you want to end up in the pokey.

For the benefit of the uninitiated '110' in OZ means kilometres (68 miles).

Same confusion sometimes at our petrol stations (gas stations to you) where there are no gallons, just litres.

Americans have a super-highway system and Australia doesn't. It's got something to do with gross domestic product, taxation from motorists being returned into the road system and the fact that Australia is the same size as the USA, but with the population of New York City.

The upshot of this is that some Aussie roads are built to US standards, but not many of them. Most are the equivalent of US Blue Roads, which is frustrating if you're in a hurry, but not so bad if you're just touring around.

Service in roadhouses is also not up to US standards – except at McDonalds.

I was sitting at a roadside diner one day when a couple of travelling Americans came in. They asked for their eggs "sunny side up" and "over and easy" respectively, along with detailed instructions on what to include, the degree of bacon crispiness, what to "hold" and what type of toast they wanted.

The amply-breasted waitress on the other side of the counter appeared to listen attentively and then committed her instructions to paper for the 'greasy spoon' wielder in the kitchen.

The result? He gave them a 'no nonsense' standard Aussie breakfast.

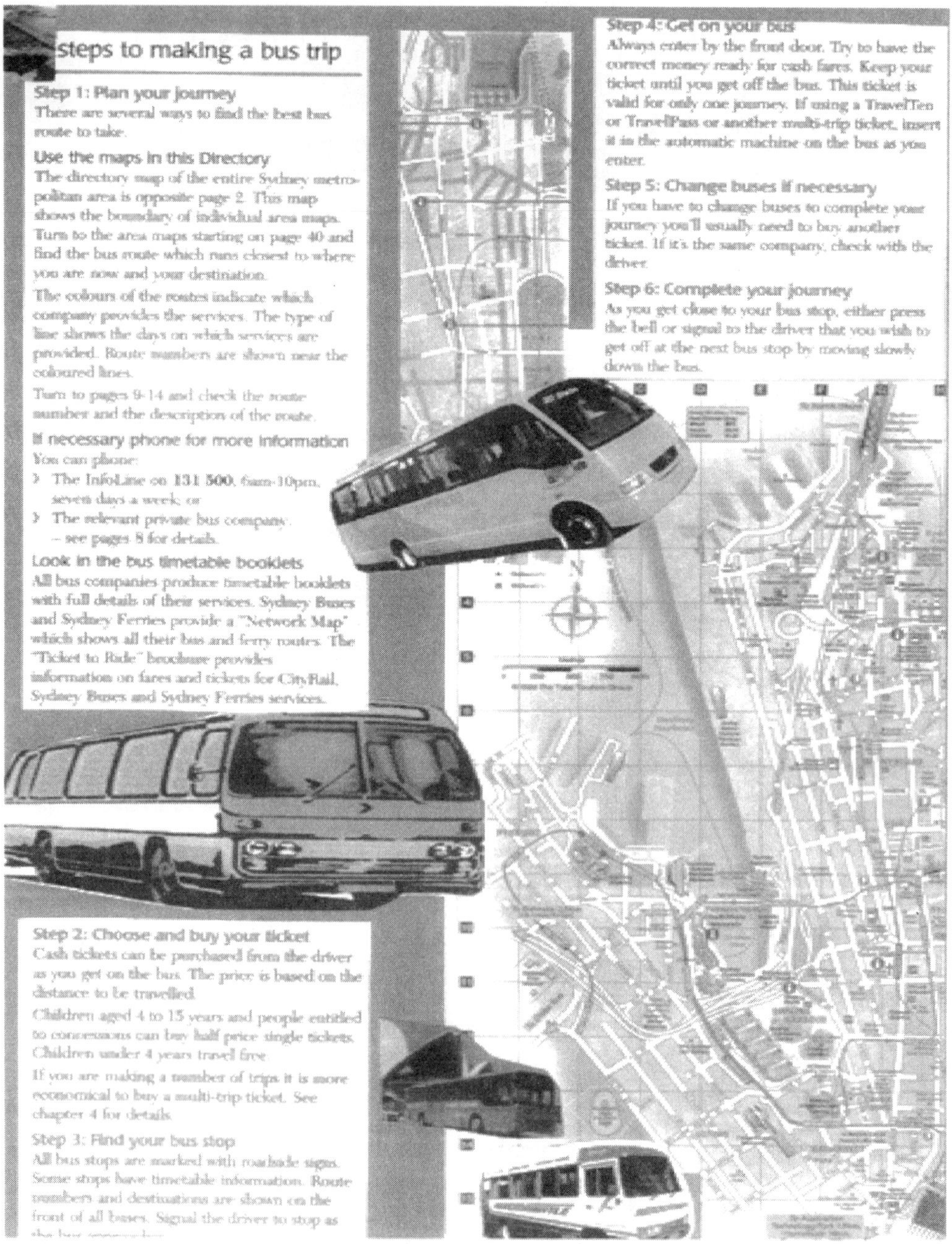

steps to making a bus trip

Step 1: Plan your journey
There are several ways to find the best bus route to take.

Use the maps in this Directory
The directory map of the entire Sydney metropolitan area is opposite page 2. This map shows the boundary of individual area maps. Turn to the area maps starting on page 40 and find the bus route which runs closest to where you are now and your destination.

The colours of the routes indicate which company provides the services. The type of line shows the days on which services are provided. Route numbers are shown near the coloured lines.

Turn to pages 9-14 and check the route number and the description of the route.

If necessary phone for more information
You can phone:

- The InfoLine on **131 500**, 6am-10pm, seven days a week; or
- The relevant private bus company – see pages 8 for details.

Look in the bus timetable booklets
All bus companies produce timetable booklets with full details of their services. Sydney Buses and Sydney Ferries provide a "Network Map" which shows all their bus and ferry routes. The "Ticket to Ride" brochure provides information on fares and tickets for CityRail, Sydney Buses and Sydney Ferries services.

Step 2: Choose and buy your ticket
Cash tickets can be purchased from the driver as you get on the bus. The price is based on the distance to be travelled.

Children aged 4 to 15 years and people entitled to concessions can buy half price single tickets. Children under 4 years travel free.

If you are making a number of trips it is more economical to buy a multi-trip ticket. See chapter 4 for details.

Step 3: Find your bus stop
All bus stops are marked with roadside signs. Some stops have timetable information. Route numbers and destinations are shown on the front of all buses. Signal the driver to stop as

Step 4: Get on your bus
Always enter by the front door. Try to have the correct money ready for cash fares. Keep your ticket until you get off the bus. This ticket is valid for only one journey. If using a TravelTen or TravelPass or another multi-trip ticket, insert it in the automatic machine on the bus as you enter.

Step 5: Change buses if necessary
If you have to change buses to complete your journey you'll usually need to buy another ticket. If it's the same company, check with the driver.

Step 6: Complete your journey
As you get close to your bus stop, either press the bell or signal to the driver that you wish to get off at the next bus stop by moving slowly down the bus.

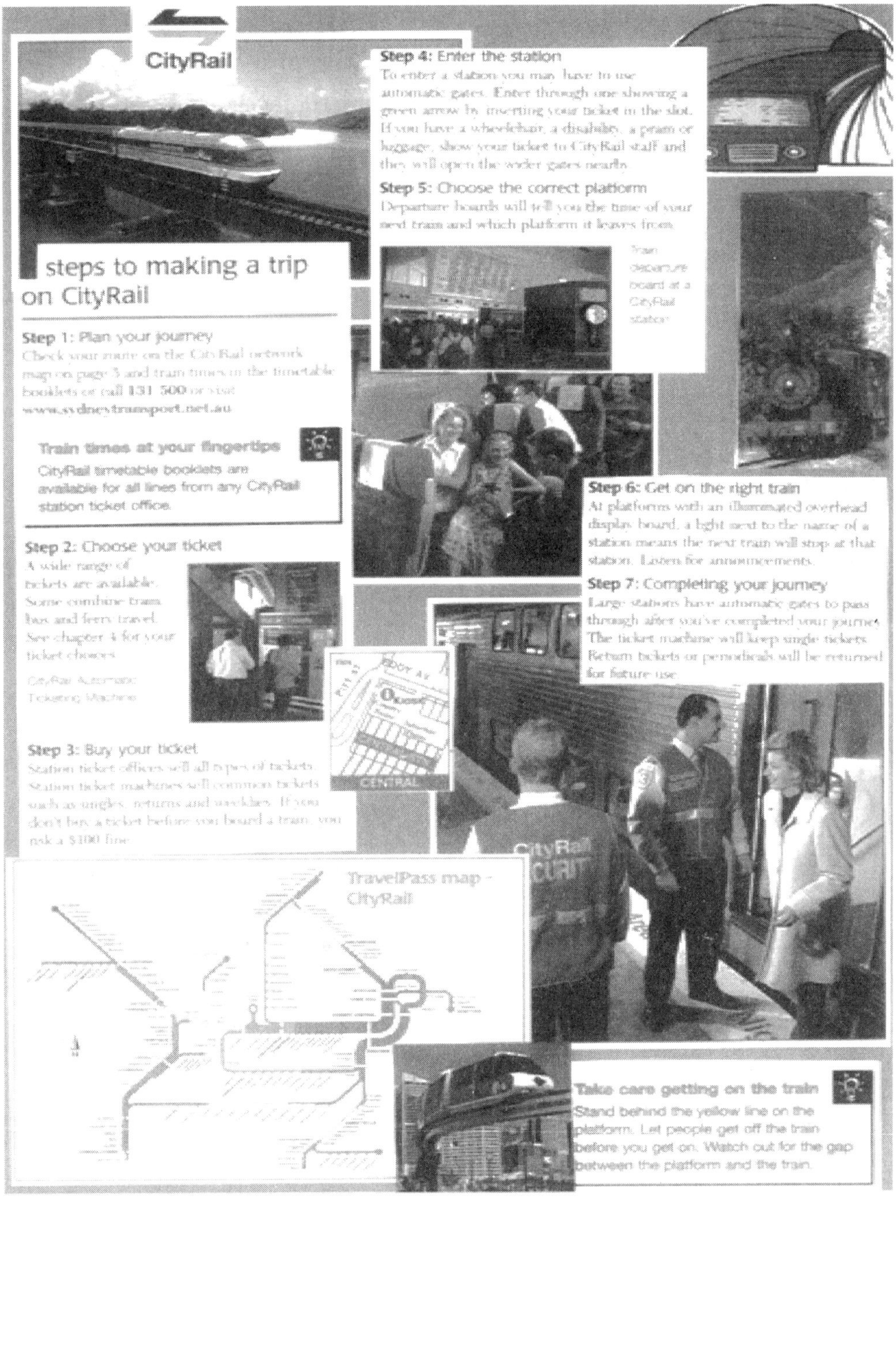

CityRail

steps to making a trip on CityRail

Step 1: Plan your journey

Check your route on the CityRail network map on page 3 and train times in the timetable booklets or call **131 500** or visit **www.sydneytransport.net.au**

Train times at your fingertips

CityRail timetable booklets are available for all lines from any CityRail station ticket office.

Step 2: Choose your ticket

A wide range of tickets are available. Some combine train, bus and ferry travel. See chapter 4 for your ticket choices.

CityRail Automatic Ticketing Machine

Step 3: Buy your ticket

Station ticket offices sell all types of tickets. Station ticket machines sell common tickets such as singles, returns and weeklies. If you don't buy a ticket before you board a train, you risk a $100 fine.

Step 4: Enter the station

To enter a station you may have to use automatic gates. Enter through one showing a green arrow by inserting your ticket in the slot. If you have a wheelchair, a disability, a pram or luggage, show your ticket to CityRail staff and they will open the wider gates nearby.

Step 5: Choose the correct platform

Departure boards will tell you the time of your next train and which platform it leaves from.

Train departure board at a CityRail station

Step 6: Get on the right train

At platforms with an illuminated overhead display board, a light next to the name of a station means the next train will stop at that station. Listen for announcements.

Step 7: Completing your journey

Large stations have automatic gates to pass through after you've completed your journey. The ticket machine will keep single tickets. Return tickets or periodicals will be returned for future use.

TravelPass map - CityRail

Take care getting on the train

Stand behind the yellow line on the platform. Let people get off the train before you get on. Watch out for the gap between the platform and the train.

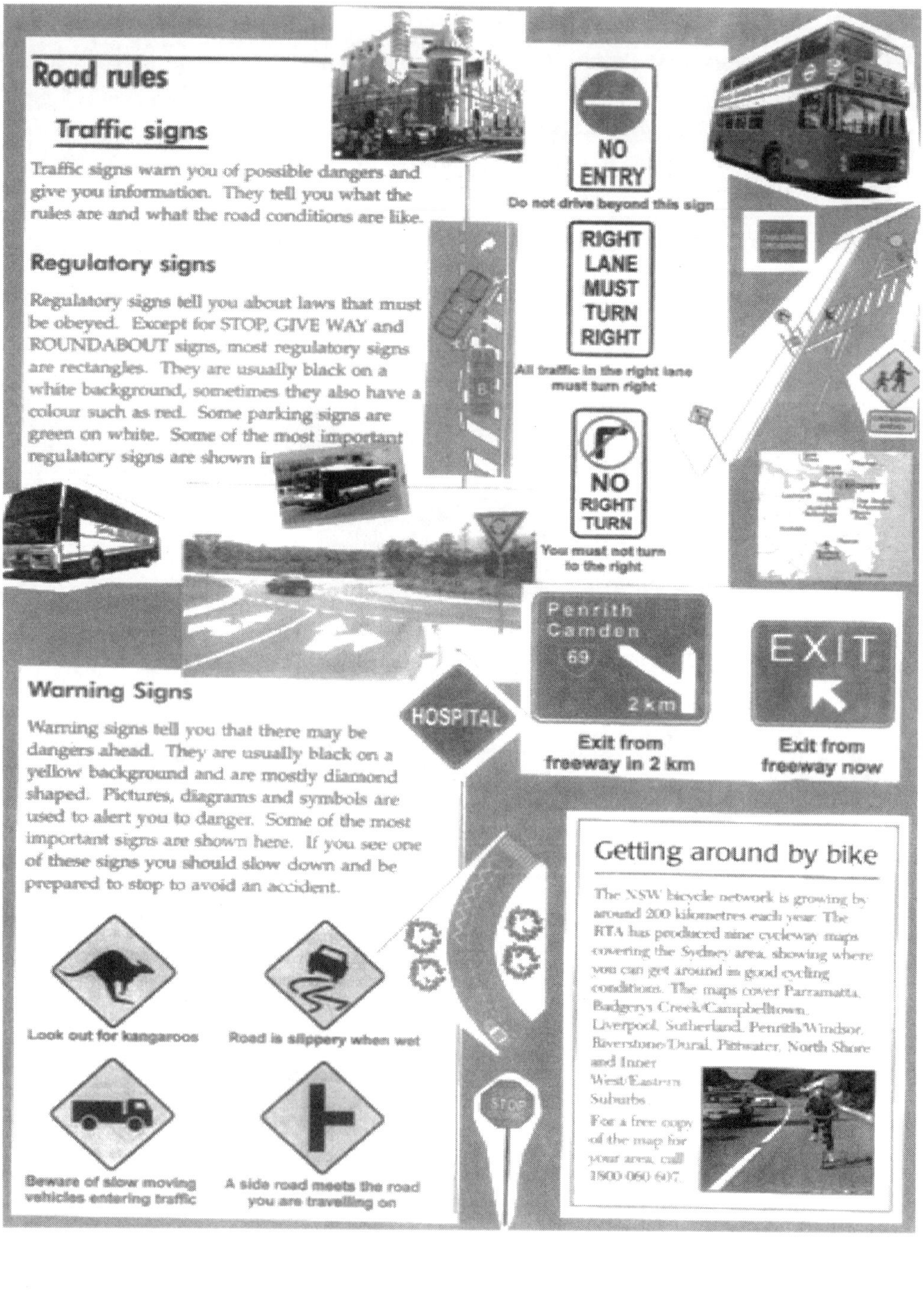

Road rules

Traffic signs

Traffic signs warn you of possible dangers and give you information. They tell you what the rules are and what the road conditions are like.

Regulatory signs

Regulatory signs tell you about laws that must be obeyed. Except for STOP, GIVE WAY and ROUNDABOUT signs, most regulatory signs are rectangles. They are usually black on a white background, sometimes they also have a colour such as red. Some parking signs are green on white. Some of the most important regulatory signs are shown in

NO ENTRY

Do not drive beyond this sign

RIGHT LANE MUST TURN RIGHT

All traffic in the right lane must turn right

NO RIGHT TURN

You must not turn to the right

Penrith Camden 69 2 km

Exit from freeway in 2 km

EXIT

Exit from freeway now

HOSPITAL

Warning Signs

Warning signs tell you that there may be dangers ahead. They are usually black on a yellow background and are mostly diamond shaped. Pictures, diagrams and symbols are used to alert you to danger. Some of the most important signs are shown here. If you see one of these signs you should slow down and be prepared to stop to avoid an accident.

Look out for kangaroos

Road is slippery when wet

Beware of slow moving vehicles entering traffic

A side road meets the road you are travelling on

STOP

Getting around by bike

The NSW bicycle network is growing by around 200 kilometres each year. The RTA has produced nine cycleway maps covering the Sydney area, showing where you can get around in good cycling conditions. The maps cover Parramatta, Badgerys Creek/Campbelltown, Liverpool, Sutherland, Penrith/Windsor, Riverstone/Dural, Pittwater, North Shore and Inner West/Eastern Suburbs.

For a free copy of the map for your area, call 1800 060 607.

SECURITY ENGLISH TERMINOLOGY

Absolute Speed	절대속도
Access control	출입통제
Access Aisle	진입로
Accessibility	접근가능성
Accessory Building	부속건물
Accident Coverage	사고보험
Acoustic Jamming	음향방해
Active Course	사용항로
Active Intelligence	유효정보
Active Runway	사용 활주로
Actual Time of Enroute	실비행시간
ADC(Aide-De-Camp)	부관
Addictive	습관성
Additive Table	난수표
Addressee	수신인
Adhesive Bandage	가제반창고
Adjoining Zone	인접지대
Advance	선발대
Advance Protection	선발경호
Advance Security	사전안전활동
Aerial Attack	공습
Aerial Chart	항공지도
Aerial Escort	공중호위
Aerial Ladder	고가사다리
Aerial Photograph(Aerophoto)	항공사진
Aerial Security	공중경호
Aeropause(Aerophobia)	비행공포증
Aerodyne	중항공기
Aerostat	경항공기
Agitation	선동
Aid Protective Area	치안강화지역
Air Alertness	대공경계
Air Cargo	항공화물
Air Guard Post	대공초소
Air Lane	항공로
Air Navigation	공중항법
Air Patrol	공중감시
Air Pickets	공중초계기
Air Sickness	비행기 멀미
Air Surveillance	대공감시
Airborne Transport	공수수송
Aircraft Arresting System	항공기제어장치
Aircraft Block Speed	항공기구간속도
Aircraft Commander(AC)	항공기 기장
Aircraft Utilization	평균비행시간
Aircraft Warning(AW)	대공경보
Airlift	탑재량
Airlift Plane	수송기
Airport Ceremony Outline	공항행사개요
Airport Facilities	공항시설
Airport Lighting System	공항야간조명시스템
Airport Passport	공항출입증
Airport Security Plan	공항 경비계획
Airport Ceremony Layout	공항행사 배치도
Airport Ceremony Outline	공항행사개요
Airport Facility	공항편의시설
Airport Size	비행장규모
Aisle Seat	통로측 좌석
Alert Emergency	비상
All Round Security	사주경계
All Weather Navigation Facility	전천후항법시설
Alma Mater	모교

Alternate Event in Case of Rain 우천시별도행사
Alternate Routes 예비통로
Altitude 고도
Ambassador 대사
Ambassador Extraordinary 특명전권대사
Ambassador's Residence 대사관저
Ammo(Ammunition) 탄약
Amnesty 사면 특사
Announcement 안내방송
Annual Message 연두교서
Anoxia 산소결핍증
Answering Machine 자동응답기
Antiabortion 임신중절반대
Antiaircraft Defense 대공방어
Antibiotic 항생제
Antidote 해독제
Anti-Government Activities 반정부 활동
Antinuclear 핵무기반대
Anti-Terror Operation 대테러작전
Antitoxin 해독제
Approach Light 야간착륙유도등
Apostate 변절자
Armored Vehicles 장갑차량
Arms Reach Principle 촉수거리의 원칙
Arresting Procedures 체포절차
Arrival Lobby 도착로비
Arrival Time 도착시간
Arson(Incendiary Crime) 방화죄
Artificial Respiration 인공호흡
Assassination 암살
Assassinator 암살자
Asset Management System 자산관리장치
Attention Strength 주의력
Audio Equipment 음향장비
Autograph Letter 친서
Automatic Alarm 자동경보
Automatic Fire 자동사격
Automatic Fire Detection 자동화재탐지
Automatic Gun 자동화기
Autopsy 검시
Auxiliary Airfield 보조비행장
Availability of Hangar 격납고가용여부
Aviation Duty 비행근무
Backdraft 화재시산소공급폭발
Backfire 맞불
Background Screening 신원조회
Baggage 화물
Baggage Cart 화물 짐수레
Baggage Convoy 화물호송
Baggage Inspection 화물검측
Baggage Transportation 화물수송
Balloon Bomb 기구폭탄
Banquet Room 연회장
Base Activities Unit 기저부대
Basic Ration 기본식량
Baton 경찰봉
Beacon 무선표지
Beneficiary 수혜자
Bill of Health 건강증명서
Black Box 비행기록장치
Black List 요주의인물일람표
Blank Ammunition 공포탄
Blind Broadcasting 맹목방송
Blockading Measure 봉쇄대책

Blood Pressure 혈압
Blood Test 혈액검사
Boarding Gate 탑승구
Boarding Pass 탑승권
Bodyguard 경호원
Bomb Disposal 폭발물처리
Bomb Dog 탐지견
Bomb Threat 폭파위협
Booking 예약
Breathing Capacity 폐활량
Bulletproof 방탄
Bulletproof Bag 방탄가방
Bulletproof Blanket 방탄담요
Bulletproof Coat (Vest) 방탄코트(조끼)
Bulletproof Podium 방탄연대
C-130 (Hercules) 공중투하중거리수송기
Cabin 객실
Cabin Service 기내서비스
Cabin Shopping 기내쇼핑
Calling Card 소개용명함
Campus Guard 대학경비원
Cannon Salute 예포
Capture 체포
Cardiopulmonary Resuscitation 심폐소생술
Career Consul 직업영사
Cargo Plane 화물수송기
Cargo Truck 화물차량
Carrying Weapon 휴대무기
Case Officer 비밀공작관
Casualty 사상자
Catering 음식물탑재
Central Intelligence Agency(CIA) 미중앙정보부

Chemical Fire Engine 화학소방차
Chief Executive Officer(CEO) 최고경영자
Chief of P.S.S. 경호실장
Chopper 헬리콥터
Cipher Code 암호통신법
City Map 시가지도
Civil Defense 민방위활동
Civil Disturbance 민간소요
Civil War 내전
Claim Tag 수화물상환증
Classified Documents 기밀문서
Clinical Diary 병상일지
Client 의뢰인
Closet 선반
Cockpit 조정석
Code Word 음어
Collect Call 수신인 지불통화
Combat Air Patrol 전투초계비행
Combustible 가연물
Commander 경찰서장
Commendation 표창
Communication Agents 통신요원
Communication Authorities 통신당국
Communication Equipment 통신기기
Communication Network 통신망
Compass 나침반
Conciliation 조정 화해
Conference 회의
Confidential Information 비밀정보
Conflict 분쟁
Conspiracy 음모
Consulate 영사관

Contact address	연락처
Containment Polish	봉쇄정책
Contrary Weather	악천후
Control Point of Traffic	교통통제점
Control Tower	관제소
Controlling Measure	통제대책
Convalescent Facility	요양시설
Convention	회의
Convoy	호송단
Convoy of Vehicles	차량호송단
Cooking Utensil	취사용구
Coordination Point	협조점
Cop	경찰관
Corruption	부패
Countermeasures	대처방법
Counter Act	차단
Counter Information	역정보
Counter Intelligence	대첩보활동
Counter Measure	대비책
Counter Terror Team	대테러팀
Crackdown	단속
Crew(Steward/ Stewardess)	승무원
Crisis Management	위기관리
Crowd Control	군중통제
Cruising Speed	순항속도
Cryptic Coloring	보호색
Current Local Time	현지시간
Custody	감금
Custom Inspection	세관검사
Customs Declaration	세관신고
Customs Procedure of Baggage	화물통관수속
Daily Mean Temperature	일일평균기온
Date of Arrival	도착일
Date of Birth	생년월일
Dead Angle	사각
Dead Zone	사각지대
Deception Communication	기만통신
Deception Installation	기만시설
Deception Operation	기만작전
Decoration	훈장 표창
Deep Pocket	자금원 부자
Defense Department	국방성
Defensive Driving	방어운전
Defensive Obstacle	방어장애물
Delegation's Baggage	수행원화물
Demonstration Operation	양동작전
Departure Lobby	출발로비
Departure Time	출발시간
Deployment of Protective Force	경호병력배치
Deputy	대리인
Destination	목적지
Detail Protection	근접경호
Detail Protective Formation	근접경호대형
Detection of VIP Vehicle	전용차량검측
Detection Security Agents	검측요원
Detonating Agent	기폭제
Detonating Assembly	기폭장치
Dignitary Protective Division	요인경호과
Diplomatic Corps	외교단
Diplomatic Mission	외교사절
Direction Finder	방향탐지기
Director of Operation Center	종합상황실장
Disaster	대참사
Disclosure	폭로

Disguise	위장술
Dispensary	외래진료실
Disposition of Force	병력배치
Diversionary Tactics	양동작전
Double Agent	이중간첩
Drug and Violent Crimes	마약폭력범죄
Drum Major	군악대장
Duty-Free Shop	면세점
Duty Post	근무초소
Duty Roster	근무편성표
Duty Runway	사용활주로
Duty Shift	근무교대
Early Warning System	조기경보체계
Easter Show	부활축제
Economy Class	보통석
Electric Facilities	전기시설
Electronic Detection	전자검측
Elevated Ladders	고가차
Emergency Call	긴급전화
Emergency Countermeasures	비상대책
Emergency Evacuation Plan	비상대피계획
Emergency Exit	비상구
Emergency Light	비상등
Emergency Line(Hot Line)	긴급통신
Emergency Measure	비상대책
Emergency Medical Technician	응급구조대원
Emergency Medical Treatment	응급치료
Emergency Power	비상전원
Emergency Room	응급실
Emergency Route	비상통로
Emergency Shelter	비상대피소
Emergency Staircase	비상계단
Employee	종사자
Employment of Ambulance	구급차 운용
Employment of Force	병력운용
Endurance Flight	항속비행
Endurance Hour	체공시간
Entrance Pass	출입증
Entrance Screening	출입통제
Entrance to the Event Site	행사장입구
Entry and Egress	출입구
Entry is Over	입장완료
Epaulettes	장교견장
Equipment and Facilities	장비 및 시설
Escape	탈출
Escort Flight	호위비행
Escort Formation	호위대형
Estimate of Security	보안판단
Evacuation	대피
Event Site Survey	행사장답사
Exclusion Zone	출입금지구역
Execution	사형집행
Exit and Entrance Procedure	출입절차
Expected Area of Crowds	군중예상운집지역
Expedition	탐험대
Expertise	전문가
Explosive Ordnance Disposal	폭발물 처리반
Explosive Detectors	폭발물탐지기
Explosives	폭발물
Extra Charge	별도요금
Extra Key	보조열쇠
Extremist	극단론자
Eyewitness	목격자
Facility Security	시설보안

Failure of Electricity	정전
False Arrest	불법체포
Fare	운임
Farewell Event	환송행사
Fellow Work Colleagues	현장동료
Fingerprint	지문
Fire Casualties	화재사상자
Fire Detector	화재감지기
Fire Drill	소방훈련
Fire Engine	소방차량
Fire Equipment	소방장비
Fire Extinguisher	소화기
Fire Fighting Equipment	소화장비
Fire Fighting Team	소방팀
Fire Hydrant	소화전
Fire Prevention	소방
Fire Prevention Equipment	소방시설
Fire-Proof Jacket	방열복
Fire Rescue Team	소방팀
Fire Service	소방
Fire Truck	소방차
Firearm Training	사격훈련
First Lady	영부인
First-Aid Kit (Case)	구급상자
Flag at Half-mast	조기
Flame Thrower	화염방사기
Flight Number	편명
Flight Operation Room	운항실
Flight Restriction	비행제한사항
Flying Time	비행시간
Follow-up Agents	후미경호
Follow-up Car(Rear Car)	후미차량
Food Inspection	검식
Food Inspector	검시관
Food Materials	식재료
Food Poisoning	식중독
Foods Prohibited	금기식품
Foreboding	예감
Forensic Science	과학수사
Formations in an Emergency	비상사태시 대형
Forum	공개토론
Freight Elevator	화물용엘리베이터
Frisk	총기소지신체수색
Fruitful Diplomacy	실리외교
Fuel Check	연료점검
Fueling Plane	급유기
Fugitive	도망자
Full Dress	정장
Funeral Service	장례식
Future-Oriented Education	미래지향교육
Gas mask	방독면
General Demeanor	품행
General Detection	일반검측
Geographical Factor	지리적위해요인
Gift Shop	기념품점
Goodwill Visit	친선방문
Gray Propaganda	회색선전
Grenade	수류탄
Ground Facility	비행장시설
Guest Quarters	영빈관
Guide Course	안내코스
Guard Duty	위병근무
Guard House	위병소
Guard Rail	교통차단기

Guard Sector	경비구역
Guide Flag	유도기
Handcuff	수갑
Handle with Care	취급주의
Hangar	격납고
Health (medical) Certificate	건강진단서
Health Screening	건강검진
Heart Failure	심장마비
Heatstroke	일사병
High Blood Pressure	고혈압
High Commissioner	고등판무관
Host	주최자
Hostage	인질
Hostile Countries	적성국
Household APPLIANCES	가정용구
Identification Screening	신원확인
Illuminating Projectile	조명탄
Immigration Card	출입국카드
Immunization	면역
Impotence	무기력
Inauguration Address	취임사
Incendiary Bomb(Shell)	소이탄
Incidents	사건
Indigestion(dyspepsia)	소화불량
Infiltrator	잠입자
Inflation Boat	공기주입고무보트
In-Flight Vulnerability	항로취약성
Inform in Advance	사전통보
Informant	정보제공자
Information and Intelligence	첩보 및 정보
Information Center	안내소
Inner Ring	내곽
Insomnia	불면증
Insurance Certificate	보험증
Intelligence Coordination	정보협조
Intelligence Officer	정보관
Internal Facilities	내부시설
International Airport	국제공항
International Call	국제전화
International Terrorists	국제테러분자
Intruder	침입자
Invitation Card	초청장
Invited Guests	초청인사
Itinerary	일정
Joint Duty	합동근무
Joint Meeting	합동회의
Joint Responsibility	합동책임
Joint Survey	합동답사
Joint Technical Search	합동검측
Jump Seat	보조의자
Jurisdiction	관할권
Keep Away	접근방지
Key Person's Profile	책임자인적사항
Kidnapping	납치
Kitchen Utensils	주방기구
Knighthood	기사도
Korean Residents	한국교민
Lachrymatory	최루제
Land	착륙
Land Bridge	육교
Land-water Car	수륙양용차
Landing Site	착륙지역
Landing Spot	착륙지점
Lavatory/ Toilet	화장실

Layout	배치
Layout of the Airport	비행장요도
Lead Agent	선도경호원
Lead Car(Vehicle)	선도차량
Leakage of Information	정보누설
Leakage of Secrets	기밀누설
Leather Goods	가죽제품
Lethal Dose	치사량
Lethargy	혼수상태
Letter of Credence	신임장
Letter of Instruction	훈령
Levels of Protection	경호등급
Liability Coverage	책임보험
License Plate Reader	차량번호판인식기
Life Jacket	구명동의
Light Automatic Gun	경기관총
Line-up Dignitaries	도열인사
Local Call	시내전화
Local Climate	지역기후
Local Food	향토음식
Lock-in	봉쇄
Long Distance Call	장거리통화
Long Range Weapon	장거리살상무기
Lost and Found	분실물취급
Lost Articles	분실물
Main Gate	정문
Man-made Disaster	자연재해
Maneuvering Protection	기동간 경호
Maneuvering Deception	기동기만
Marginal Weather	악천후
Marine	해병
Mass Destruction	대량살상
Mass Observation	여론조사
Mass Transit	대량수송수단
Massacre	대학살
Material Factor	물적위해요소
Medical Inspection	검역
Medical Jurisprudence	법의학
Meeting at the Summit	정상회담
Memoir	회고록
Memorandom	비망록
Metal Detector	금속탐지기
Meteorological Observation	기상관측
Meteorological Summary	기상개황
Minister	장관
Minister Pleipotentiary	전권공사
Mobile Person	순찰대원
Mobile Security	기동경호
Mobilization Plan	동원계획
Mobilization to the Site	행사장출동
Money Order	우편환
Motion Detector	동작감지기
Motorcade Alignment	차량정렬
Motorcade Formation	차량대형
Movement Route	기동로
Mr. Ambassador	대사
Mr. President	대통령님
National Anthem	애국가
National Cemetery	국립묘지
National Friendship	국교
National Guest	국빈
National Intelligence	국가정보
National Power	국력
National Security	국가안전보장

National Strategy	국가전략	Out-of-Date	시대에 뒤진
Nationality	국적	Outlet	콘센트
Natural Disaster	자연재해	Overpower	압도하다
Nerve Cell	신경세포	Oxygen Gas Mask	산소마스크
Network of Roads	도로망	Pain Killer	진통제
Next Schedule	차기계획	Panel Discussion	공개토론회
No Trespassing	출입금지	Par Avion / By Air Mail	항공우편
Non-Smoking Section	금연석	Parachute	낙하산
Oath	선서	Parking Lot Control	주기장통제
Obligation	책무	Passenger Ticket	항공권
Occupied	사용중	Passengers Inspection	출입사열
Occurrence	발생	Passport	여권
Offenders	침입자	Passport Number	여권번호
Off-guard	비번	Patrol Car	순찰차
Off-limit Area(Restricted Area)	통제구역	Patrol Duties	순찰의무
Officer in Charge	책임자	Patrol Routes	순찰경로
Official Courtesies	공식적예의	Patron	고객
Official Event	공식행사	Pavement Condition	도로포장상태
Official Visit	공식방문	Performance of Duties	임무수행
Old Case	전례	Person-to-Person Call	지명통화
One Way Fare	편도요금	Personal Background	인적사항
One Way Ticket	편도 항공권	Personal Belongings	소지품(휴대품)
Open Diplomacy	공개외교	Personal Factor	인적 위해요소
Open Sea	공해	Personal Property	개인소유물
Operation of K9 Unit	탐지견운용	Petition	청원
Operation of Reaction Team	기동타격대운용	Physical Training	체력단련
Operation of VIP Reserve Car	VIP 예비차운용	Pickpocket	소매치기
Operational Directions	작전지휘	Place of Birth	출생지
Operational Supervision	작전감독	Platform	단상
Operator	전화교환원	Podium	연단
Ornaments	장식품	Position of Our Security Agents	아측경호원위치
Outer Ring	외곽	Possibility of Air Attack	공중위해가능성

Potential Criminals 감시대상자
Potentially Rebellious Behaviour 잠재적불순행위
Power of Command 명령권
Precipitation 강수량
Preliminary Safety Measures 사전안전조치
Preliminary Test 사전점검
Preliminary Threat Reports 사전위협보고
Premises 건물, 부동산
Prescription 처방전
Presidential Aircraft 전용기
Presidential Medical Doctor 대통령 주치의
Presidential Aircraft Security 대통령전용기경비
Presidential Secretariat 비서실
Presidential Security Agent 대통령 경호원
Press Control 보도요원통제
Press Conference 기자회견
Press Corps 기자단
Press Equipment 보도기자재
Preventive Measures 방호대책
Prime Minister 수상
Principal (Protectee) 피경호인
Prior Permission 사전승인
Private Patrol Officer 청원순찰경찰
Prohibited Article 반입금지품목
Proliferation 확산
Property 재산
Proposition Bill 건의안
Protection While VIP Walking 도보간 경호
Protective Deception 경호기만
Protective Environment 경호환경
Protective Information 경호첩보
Protective Intelligence 경호정보
Protective Security Plan 경호경비계획
Protective Service 신변보호업무
Protective Techniques 경호기술
Protocol 의전
Protocol Call 의례적방문
Protocol Secretary 의전비서관
PSS(Presidential Security Service) 대통령경호실
Pulse 맥박
Quantity of Holding Fuel 연료보유량
Radar Spotting 레이더탐지
Radio 무전기
Radio Auditor Equipment 무선감시장비
Radio Frequencies 무전주파수
Radio Navigation 무선항법
Radio Silence 무선사용금지
Radioactive Waste 방사성폐기물
Railway Crossing 철도건널목
Railway Escort 철도호송
Ransom 몸값
Rate of Fire 발사속도
Reaction Team 기동타격대
Reactor 원자로
Rear Guard Car 후미경호차
Rear Trap 후미트랩
Rebellious Behavior 불순행위
Receipt 영수증
Receiver 영접자
Receiving Line 영접열
Recreation Facilities 휴양시설
Refuge 피난자 망명자
Registered Mail 등기우편
Registration Card 숙박신고서

Rehabilitation	복구	Safety Shelter	비상대피소
Rehearsal	예행연습	Safety Room	대피소
Reinforce Spot-Check	검문강화	Salute Guns(Gun-Salute)	예포
Reinforcement Plan	보강계획	Salvage Company	구조대
Repeater Base	무선중계기	Salvation	구제
Rescue Crew	구조원	Sanitary Inspection	위생검사
Rescue Vehicles	구난차	Scale of Duty Force	근무병력규모
Reservation	예약	Schedule Board	발착일람표
Reserve Aircraft	예비기	Screening Efficiency	요인은폐효율
Reserve Airport	예비공항	Screening Methods	검색방안
Reserve Car	예비차	Search Activities by Our Side	아측 검측활동
Reserved Seat Ticket	지정석권	Search and Rescue Service	재해구난업무
Residence Security	숙소경비	Searching Control	탐조조정장치
Residence Facilities	숙소편의시설	Seat Arrangement	승차조율(좌석배치도)
Responsibility for Security	경호책임	Secret Badge	비표
Restricted Area	제한지역	Secretary Interpreter	통역관
Restricted Traffic	통행제한	Secure Area	안전구역
Right of Self-Defense	자위권	Security Agent	경호원
Riot Leader	집회주모자	Security Arrangement	안전조치
Road Closed	통행금지	Security Check	보안검사
Road Maintenance	도로정비	Security Command Post	경호지휘소
Road Net	도로망	Security Evaluation Conference	경호평가회의
Roadside Security	연도경호	Security Forces	경호인력
Round Trip Fare	왕복요금	Security Guard	경호원
Round Trip Ticket	왕복항공권	Security Intelligence	경호정보
Runway	활주로	Security Measures	안전대책
Safe House	은신처	Security Meeting	경호관계관회의
Safety Box	귀중품보관소	Security Procedure	경호절차
Safety Officer	안전관리자	Security Support Vehicles	경호지원차량
Safety Precaution	안전수칙	Seismograph	지진계
Safety Sector	안전구역	Serial Number	총기번호
Safety Security	안전확보	Service Shift	근무교대

Set-up of the Control Center 통제소설치
Shelter 대피소
Shift Schedule 근무교대계획
Short Range Weapon 단거리살상무기
Shoulder Insignia 어깨견장
Side Effect 부작용
Sign Post 이정표
Signaling Method 신호방식
Signature 서명
Simplified Procedure 간이통과
Site Survey 행사장답사
Size of Force 병력규모
Size of Welcoming Crowd 환영객규모
Sound Off(Warning) 경고
Souvenir Shop 기념품점
Special Aircraft 특별기
Special Security Team 전담경호대
Sporting Celebrity 스포츠유명인사
Squad 경찰분대
Static Guard 초소경비원
Staff Car 수행원차량
Stairway 층계
Stand-by Ambulance 구급차대기
Stand-by Area 대기지역
Stand-by Car 대기차량
Stand-by Power Supply 예비전원
Stand-by Radio 무전개방대기
Star and Stripes 성조기
State Department 국무성
State Minister 국무장관
Steady State 정상상태
Step Car 트랩차량
Strike Force 특별임무팀
Subject Under Close Watch 요시찰인
Submarine Screen 잠수함경계
Summit Conference 정상회담
Sunrise and Sunset Time 일출 일몰시간
Support Ability 지원능력
Support Equipment 지원장비
Support Service 지원업무
Supreme Command 통수권
Surveillance Team 감시조
Suspect 불순용의자
Suspect under Surveillance 감시대상자
Switchboard 전화교환대
Table Manner 식사예절
Take Off 이륙
Task Force 특수임무기동대
Taxi Guidance Light 유도도로등
Taxi Stand 택시승강장
Technical Detection 검측
Telescope 망원경
Terminal Building 공항청사
Terror 테러 공포
Threat Analysis 위해분석
Threat Factor 위해요소
Ticket Window 매표구
Time Difference 시차
Toll Road 유료도로
Towel Disposal 휴지통
Traffic Control 교통통제
Traffic Controlling Vehicles 경호순찰차량
Traffic Patrol 교통순찰
Traffic Volume 교통량

Transfer Gate	갈아타는 곳	VIP Aircraft	VIP 특별전용기
Transformer Station	변전소	VIP Cargo	VIP 화물
Transit Passenger	통과여객	VIP Luggage Vehicle	VIP 화물차량
Traveler's Checks	여행자수표	VIP Room(VIP Lounge)	귀빈실
Trespass	불법침입	VISA	비자 사증
Tug Car(Tractor)	항공기견인차	Visual Alarm System	시각경보설비
Turbulence	난기류	Visual Image Recognition	화상인식
Turmoil	혼란	Voltage Transformation	전압변형
Uncoverage	노출지역	Volunteer Fire Department	의용소방대
Under Construction	공사중	Vulnerable Area	취약지역
Uneven Ground	요철지형	Waiting Room(Lounge)	대합실
Unfair Competition	불공정경쟁	Walking Alignment	도보대형
Uniformed Police	정복경찰	Walking Formation	도보대형
United Nations(UN)	국제연합	Wanted Man	지명수배자
Unpredictable	예측할수없는	Water Quality	수질상태
Updated Internal Report	최근입수정보	Weather Forecast	기상예보
Urgent Telegram	긴급전보	Weather Satellite	기상위성
Vacant	비어있음	Weather Station	기상대
Valuables	귀중품	Welcoming Crowds	환영인파
Vandalism	예술문화파괴	Welcoming Dignitaries	영접자
Vantage Point	유리한 지점	Welcoming Events	환영행사
Vehicle Chart	차량편성표	Welcoming Parties	영접인사
Vehicle Maintenance	차량정비	Weapons of Mass Destruction	대량살상무기
Vehicular Assault	차량습격	West Point	미 육군사관학교
Venue	현장	While Walking	보행간
Ventilation	환기장치	Window Seat	창측 좌석
Ventilating System	공조체제	Windshield	앞유리
Venue	회합장소	Wireless Sensor	무선감지기
Veteran	퇴역재향군인	Witness	증인
Vice president	부통령 부사장	Yeoman of the Guard	친위병
Victim	희생자		

Security English

인쇄 / 2013년 11월 18일
발행 / 2013년 11월 25일

저 자 / 신홍섭 · 김명영
발행인 / 김 창 석
발행처 / 홍 익 출 판 사

대구광역시 중구 삼덕 3가 245-2
(053) 421-6700, 427-3627
등록 1987년 10월 26일 제1-107호

정가 13,000원

ISBN 978-89-7826-251-4 93740

이 도서의 국립중앙도서관 출판시도서목록(CIP)은 서지정보유통지원시스템 홈페이지(http://seoji.nl.go.kr)와 국가자료공동목록시스템(http://www.nl.go.kr/kolisnet)에서 이용하실 수 있습니다. (CIP제어번호 : CIP2013024499)